GENDER IS NOT
A SYNONYM FOR WOMEN

GENDER AND POLITICAL THEORY:
NEW CONTEXTS

Series Editor
Judith Grant
University of Southern California

Editorial Board

GENDER
IS NOT A SYNONYM
FOR WOMEN

Terrell Carver

LYNNE
RIENNER
PUBLISHERS

BOULDER
LONDON

Published in the United States of America in 1996 by
Lynne Rienner Publishers, Inc.
1800 30th Street, Boulder, Colorado 80301

and in the United Kingdom by
Lynne Rienner Publishers, Inc.
3 Henrietta Street, Covent Garden, London WC2E 8LU

Library of Congress Cataloging-in-Publication Data
Carver, Terrell.
    Gender is not a synonym for women / Terrell Carver.
      p. cm.—(Gender and political theory)
    Includes bibliographical references and index.
    ISBN 1-55587-320-0 (hc : alk. paper)
    1. Feminist theory—Political aspects. 2. Gender identity—
political aspects. I. Title. II. Series.
HQ1190.C38 1996
305.42'01—dc20   95-33095
                                                                        CIP

British Cataloguing in Publication Data
A Cataloguing in Publication record for this book
is available from the British Library.

Printed and bound in the United States of America

       The paper used in this publication meets the requirements
 ∞ of the American National Standard for Permanence of
       Paper for Printed Library Materials Z39.48-1984.

    5   4   3   2   1

For
Roger

Contents

Acknowledgments

I am grateful to the following publishers and journals for their kind permission to reprint edited and revised versions of previously published material: in Chapter 2, *History of Political Thought* for "Engels's Feminism," vol. 6, no. 3 (1985), pp. 479–489; and *masculinities* for "Theorizing Men in Engels's *Origin of the Family*," vol. 2, no. 1 (1994), pp. 67–77. In Chapters 3 and 4, *The Journal of Political Science* for "Methodological Issues in Writing a Political Biography," vol. 20 (1992), pp. 3–13; and Macmillan Press, London, and St. Martin's Press, New York, for *Friedrich Engels: His Life and Thought*, 1989, repr. 1991, pp. 145–171.

In addition I express my thanks to participants in various workshops, conferences, and lecture audiences for responding so helpfully, if sometimes against the grain: For Chapter 1, Western Conference for the Study of Political Thought (University of Bristol), February 1993; European Consortium for Political Research, Joint Sessions (University of Leiden), April 1993; Political Studies Association, Annual Conference (Leicester University), April 1993. For Chapter 2, American Political Science Association, Annual Meeting (New Orleans), September 1985; Department of Political Science, Public Lecture, University of Virginia, Charlottesville, November 1985; Department of Political Science, University of Minnesota, Minneapolis, May 1986. For Chapters 3 and 4, British Sociological Association, Theory Group Conference on Masculinity (Bradford University), September 1988; Political Studies Association, Marxism Group (Trent Polytechnic, Nottingham), September 1988; Department of History, University College, Swansea, December 1989; European Consortium for Political Research, Joint Sessions (Bochum University), April 1990. For Chapter 5, European Consortium for Political Research, Joint Sessions (University of Limerick), April 1992; International Political Science Association, Research Committee on Political Philosophy (London School of Economics), May 1992; International Political Science Association, XVI World Congress (Berlin), August 1994.

Finally, I would like to record particular thanks to two individuals who listened to me with tremendous patience and then told me what they thought with unmissable frankness: Anna Jonásdottír and Kathy Jones. I only hope that they can find time to give me the same again, please.

T. C.

Acknowledgments

Introduction

Who writes? For whom is the writing being done? In what circumstances?
These, it seems to me, are the questions whose answers provide us with the
ingredients making for a politics of interpretation.   —Said 1985, 135

This book is an essay in the politics of interpretation. It looks at how politics is currently interpreted, and at how these interpretations are constructed. It also interprets material that is political, one way or another, and as it does so, my own political views undoubtedly emerge. The chapters were originally papers, talks, or lectures for various audiences at gatherings framed in ways that, inevitably, I did not determine, though I certainly chose to write to the stated themes. Much of the material from which this book was written thus has found an audience already. I hope that in reworking and rethinking this material as a book, some of the issues I have been exploring will reach different audiences on terms that are more my own. I have certainly been able to bring out common themes and follow through on them in ways that could never have emerged at any individual venue.

In this book I employ multiple perspectives. I define a perspective as a question that begins to frame an answer, in that it sets the opening terms of discussion; it gets us started on inquiry and interpretation. But the question does not determine the answer at the outset, because developing answers is an exploratory process. I hope that I have the reader's patience while I undertake these explorations. I think that the questions I address are interesting, and the explorations worthwhile.

Among the perspectives employed, I particularly draw the reader's attention to those of feminist theory, which I define as "theorizations of women's oppression"; and gender studies, which I define as "investigations into the ways that sex and sexuality become power relations in society," where *sex* is male or female and *sexuality* is sexual behavior. No doubt these are somewhat idiosyncratic and less than completely informative definitions, but I offer them to hint at what to expect as the book unfolds. I have a particular project that has emerged from within both perspectives, namely a

1

focus on men as problematic in two respects: their power over women; and their use of gender in society. My aim is to develop this project in the context of political theory, broadly conceived.

Political theory is not, in my view, conceived broadly enough in most cases. Or rather it rests too comfortably, in many of its manifestations, on presumptions that need investigating. Thus, one of the things I do in this book is to treat political theory as a culturally transmitted artifact, whose peculiar characteristics are made visible in certain ways. When we consider theory as a cultural object, or scholarly tradition, any attempt to separate theory as such or contemporary theory from its history (generally conceptualized as "great thinkers" and "great books") is bound to fail. Too many standard terms have too much academic resonance for this commonplace move to succeed. Doctrines of individual rights and representative government always have Locke and J. S. Mill hovering in the background, and economic approaches to social conditions and political institutions always draw on Hobbes and Marx. This is not to say that political theory is uncritical commentary—most often it is precisely the reverse. But great thinkers and great books are essential locaters in any conceptual map, however close to them, or however distant from them, the ideas are intended to be.

It is therefore my intention to make the very construction of political theory problematic. Great thinkers and great books are inevitably framed in biographical terms, and how these biographies are constructed, not just in detail but *as biography,* bears investigation. Hence, I am concerned in this book with questions of genre, and how genre influences our reception of theoretical ideas. I am also concerned with the way that meanings within genre are characteristically derived and transmitted, namely as *stories* or *narratives.* Neither of these terms is easy to define, but I take them to refer to linguistic constructions that are longer than simple propositions and characteristically have a beginning, a middle, and an end. The end, of course, may be the end of the narration, rather than the end of the story.

In making the construction and transmission of political theory problematic, I have to utilize illustrative material, as abstract discussion would soon wear thin. Theory always has to be about something, and it always needs exemplification. That said, I do not embark on anything like a literature review of great books and great thinkers, nor do I think such a review necessary to prove my point. Instead I explore at length certain episodes in theory and in politics that interest me, and that I think will interest at least some of my readers some of the time. As I have been concerned with the ideas of and biographical frames for Karl Marx and Friedrich Engels for a good many years, I hope that it is an advantage for the reader that most of my illustrative material comes from that quarter, as most of us know, or think we know, something about them, their ideas, and their lives. Thus, Chapters 2, 3, and 4 derive from detailed researches on Engels and Marx, though my intention is to use these materials illustratively. Chapter 2 deals with a classic theorization of the family, Chapter 3 with the way that biographies of great thinkers are constructed, and Chapter 4 with the way that a singular gendered narrative has gripped biographers themselves as they write. But there are also contemporary references in my analytical material that are more than indirect or passing, such as Chapter 5 on the Clarence Thomas–Anita Hill hearings of 1991. There I explore the self-conscious use of complex, multiple, gendered narratives by political actors (who actually "acted" on TV) in the context of democratic politics and popular culture, and how this was represented in a selected media source over a few weeks.

I make no apology for dwelling at greater length on what seems a specialist interest located deep in the past (in Chapters 2, 3, and 4), rather than accessibly in the present (as in Chapter 5). Indeed, the present/past distinction is really a distancing device employed to restrict the politics of interpretation illicitly. What is in the present is constructed interpretatively from claims about the past, using terms derived from past discourse as it is culturally transmitted. The present is necessarily only the past as far as it has yet occurred. The past exists as a matter of interpreted experience for each of us, and interpretations of the interpretations others put to us. Strictly speaking, the present moment is always retrospective. Thus, a line of exclusion between a presumed present and a knowable past is arbitrary in the first instance (when exactly is the present? the last second, minute, hour, day, week, year?). And in the second instance, the present/past distinction is effectively political, in that it declares some areas of interpretative discourse out of bounds, or off-limits, or of only marginal interest. Material is said to be "merely historical" or "too far back."

There are no convincing reasons, then, for putting nineteenth-century figures, for example, into a different world merely because they are long dead or because their concerns are presumed to be considerably different from ours. (Anyway, who exactly are we?) While one wants to avoid anachronism, there are in a sense worse mistakes available when looking at politics that is nearer our own time. Being near in time to events does not guarantee interpretative authenticity, nor does being remote in time produce absolute otherness or blank incomprehension. Interpretation is negotiation with the material, with one's audience (even if only in one's imagination), and with oneself, as lines of thought emerge.

One line of thought that emerges strongly in my mind is that recent work in the sociology of masculinities has something to say to political theorists about their trade. Insofar as there is a literature review in this book, that is where it lies. Recent sociology derived from Foucault has begun to expand our notions of power in society—where it is and how it works. And feminisms have begun to upset the traditional distinctions between public or private and political or nonpolitical, and the way these terms are mapped onto each other. It seems to me that after these developments men are going to look different. While this has, of course, already happened in various ways within feminist theory, there is always room to move the discussion along, using material that is not yet commonly cited.

As there is a feminist reading of "private woman," I am aiming at a reading of "private man," in that feminists rightly argue that what women do and suffer in the private realm is in fact political and in need of public debate. Moving private man into the political foreground reinforces the feminist critique of masculine violence, domination, and privilege by looking at what men fail to do altogether, what they claim to do symbolically rather than carry out practically, and what role their sexualities play in their collective and individual constructions of power. The public realm itself can also be conceived as a private realm for men, so the ambiguities of the supposedly commonsensical public/private dichotomy become on my reading ever more varied and politically charged. Moreover, masculinity itself becomes plural and complex, and the feminist reading of classic texts in political theory as generically masculine becomes problematic. These texts must now be seen as normative constructs against a background of suppressed and varied behavior—other masculinities.

It also seems to me that it is important to move these kinds of discussion about men into the mainstream/malestream of academic and scholarly work. In my experience of this milieu I have detected not only ignorance of what feminist theorizing has accomplished but also complacency with respect to feminist theorizing as an activity; a complacency that resides in a view that feminist theorizing is always, necessarily, and most usefully done by women, for women, about women. This could perhaps be summarized as a "(Separate but) Equal Opportunities" view of affairs that "lets the girls get on with it." Wendy Brown once commented publicly (if I remember rightly!) that feminist theorists would have to address mainstream/malestream political theory as such, changing its terms of reference and doing it differently, otherwise feminist theorists would always represent "Mrs. Political Theory," with all that that false honorific implies.

Perhaps I might be allowed one further illustrative anecdote, though I do my best to disguise the identity of my interlocutor. A male colleague in political science once explained that his work could not include women political leaders, because as a matter of fact there weren't any in his field of study. He apologized to all that his work regrettably "had no *gender* dimension." My immediate and no doubt overly forthright response was, "Gender is not a synonym for women!" and hence came the title of this book. One of the obvious reasons, of course, that there were no women political leaders to be found in that context is precisely the working of gender relations with respect to women. But it was also the case, as emerged in discussion, that gender relations of masculinities, as practiced among men, played a large role in the formation of the political relations that ensured the subordination and loyalty of some men to other men, and the concomitant exclusion of women.

In many contexts one finds that a reference to gender is a reference to women, as if men, males, and masculinities were all unproblematic in that regard—or perhaps simply nothing to do with gender at all. This can readily become a way of making women problematic, once again, in a way that marginalizes them as a problem and leaves men where they have always been, doing pretty much what they like—or, more accurately, what some of them like. On the whole there have been only minimal concessions in power relations from men to women, and none at all in the basic construction of gendered (that is, power-ridden) identities derived rather incoherently from presumptions about sex and sexuality. These identities, or perhaps rather identity claims, are the real stuff of the asymmetrical social relationships we have inherited. Few people, if any, really have these identities with utter consistency and conviction. Rather, they claim them as they are performed, and in doing so establish the symbolic codes from which disciplinary practices emerge (Butler 1990).

In the common parlance of recent times, *gender* has also become a euphemism for *sex,* that is, male or female, M or F, man or woman, as biologically, socially, and legally defined. These definitions, though, are hardly unambiguous. In doctrines of family, parenthood, and personal dignity, considerations of individual preference and social functionality begin to crosscut the commonplace stereotyping on which our elaborations of the two supposedly opposite yet corequisite sexes are based. This synonymy of gender and sex seems a step backward, or at least it marks a kind of inertia. It constantly reinscribes the supposedly obvious and supposedly well-understood categories *male and female, men and women,* back into political ideas, just when these ideas are starting to be really problematic, politically interesting, and interestingly complex. Why map gender onto sex as one-to-one, just when the term was helping to make visible the ambiguities of sexuality, orientation, choice, and change that have been undercover for centuries? Indeed, modern technologies of the body, and modern methods of political mobilization, have rendered these questions not just visible but pressing within the media, the institutional apparatus of courts and legislatures, and all the professions in society.

A one-to-one mapping of gender onto a commonplace categorization of sex as male/female is overly simple, even with respect to biology and medicine, as there are chromosomal variations and syndromes, not to mention morphological ones, that create genuinely ambiguous individuals. Even supposing that "normality" with respect to the M/F distinction (as medically and socially enforced) is good enough for most analytical purposes, why limit *gender* to a restatement of that? The term was coined to do more than restate the (supposedly) obvious, by decoupling (simplified) biology from (stereotyped) behavior. Gender was taken to be the way that sex was expressed in society in terms of behavior, masculine or feminine. Feminine males and masculine females were then categorized and made problematic within psychoanalytic, psychological, or sociological theories of normality and development.

Discourses and practices of toleration and liberation have to some extent replaced the more sinister approaches and institutions that historical and sociological work on the human sciences have exposed. There is yet more room in life for discourses of variation or difference. Indeed, it seems to me that we simply do not know how many genders there are, as the answer must vary according to what is assumed about sex and sexuality before any particular concept of gender is constructed.

For instance, if there are normal or characteristic ways of being of the male or female sex, called masculine and feminine, and if these are socially learned rather than biologically determined, then there are four genders, rather than two, as masculine men, masculine women, feminine women, and feminine men become logically possible and empirically observable. If gender is the way that sexuality is expressed between the sexes, then perhaps there are two genders, heterosexuality and homosexuality (or three, if celibacy is an option), on the assumption that these categories include both males and females, depending on whether sexuality is M to F and F to M (heterosexuality), or M to M and F to F (homosexuality). Alternatively, perhaps there are four or six genders, as the lineup might then be heterosexual men, heterosexual women, homosexual women, homosexual men, celibate women, and celibate men. Perhaps historically there were three genders (heterosexual men, heterosexual women, celibates) or four (heterosexual men, heterosexual women, celibate women, celibate men), before homosexuality as a sexual identity was developed, or at least a sexual identity we would recognize as homosexual or the social actors themselves would identify as such (Weeks 1985). Adding bisexuality, as either one further gender or two sexually differentiated genders, runs the total up further (Evans 1993).

In terms of object of desire (male or female), perhaps there are two genders, one encompassing heterosexual women and homosexual men (both of whom desire men), and the other encompassing heterosexual men and homosexual women (who desire women). The former is actually a well-known combination as "best friends," whereas the latter does not seem to have attained much social reality or visibility that I know of. If bisexuals are added, then in terms of object of desire they are definitely one gender unto themselves, as the differentiation into women who desire women and men, and men who desire women and men seems rather pointless, as genital identity seems transcended on both sides of the equation.

Once the mapping of gender is turned from bodily organs to objects of desire, whether human or otherwise, or to performance and dressing up, the variations and possibilities move swiftly toward infinity. How one defines the bounds of sexuality is by no means unambiguous. This is relevant, for example, even to an activity that is often presented as somehow asexual and only guiltily of the body, namely parenting. This then raises issues of power and politics. If gender is part of a political identity, a group basis for political coalitions, a field of individual interest where people find common cause in similarity, perhaps *parent* is itself a gender, transcending the bodily differences that are usually identified as not just sexual, but opposite.

Considerations of difference can also be relevant here, as women in feminist politics were not the first to discover. But this immediately raises the question of similarity against which difference is supposed to be pertinent. Class and race/ethnicity among women are points of reference from which quite different notions of gender politics were constructed in terms of substantial demands and coalition strategies. The notion of gender politics as necessarily a politics of sexual polarization has been made highly problematic: could it be that the gender politics of working-class women should be oriented away from issues of male domination and toward solidarity with working-class men in an anti-imperialist struggle? Perhaps "the masculine" as a threat to feminist politics is correctly located in rich, white, capitalist societies, and not in "men of color" in any significant way?

If gender is tied to gender politics, rather than to individualized conceptions of sex and sexuality, then perhaps privileged white men and poor exploited men are in different genders as political subjects, as well as political objects? Gender politics among men is not a topic that often surfaces in political theory. It works to divide men as men and, when divided, to draw them together in ways that may be hierarchical or egalitarian, "homosocial" or homoerotic, within the divisions that are created around sex and sexuality (Hearn and Collinson 1994). Gender politics among men is thus by no means always in opposition to women or to conceptions of women's interests. One of my objectives in this book is to explore (just a little) the ways that men are divided (and perforce united) by class or race/ethnicity such that they are constructed differently as men or masculine subjects in their own behavior, and in the way their behavior is interpreted by others in the political realm.

On the one hand, such naturalized or commonplace categories as sex, gender, class, and race/ethnicity are manipulated in politics to construct inclusions and exclusions with respect to groups, an inside and an outside with respect to a border or boundary line, and various maps of identity and difference—so that allies and enemies, partners and opponents, powerful and powerless are produced as societies apparently function. But on the other hand, these constructions, despite all the disciplinary apparatuses employed, map poorly onto the varieties of experience that individuals can still manage to generate in living their lives as human agents, and that interpreters such as political theorists can construct as a recovery. It is up to each of us to make our own interpretations and to generate our own purposive context, though we cannot always do this just as we like. That is why this book is not a typology of fact, but an exploration of how *gender* and *women* have been made to interact in political theory as currently constructed.

In Chapter 1 I situate my concerns within the current debates of political theory, in that I address feminist politics and theory, and theories and studies of gender. In particular I address theories of gender that have been developed in a postmodernist frame. To that context I introduce the sociology of masculinities, distinguishing this carefully from men's studies, men's consciousness activities, and "the men's movement." I think that the sociological literature on masculinity/ies can usefully be brought to bear on issues raised in feminist theory and gender studies, and I briefly review aspects of this literature of particular interest to political theorists. In doing this, I focus on the human or universal subject in political theory, and on how this idealized person has been constructed—and deconstructed.

These deconstructions reveal the politicized character of the public/private distinction in traditional political theories. In particular this discursive subject appears, or can be shown to appear, as both male or masculine and degendered or neutered in various scholarly sources and popular discourse. I explore this apparent contradiction, which feminist theory correctly identifies in political discourse and practice, as a discursive device in gender politics.

As a representation of humanity, this abstract individual is certainly not a woman, but not therefore really a man. While it abstracts away from specifically female aspects of reproduction, it also abstracts away from sexuality altogether, as well as other aspects of the body and bodily differences. Moreover, the dynamics of the dominant masculinities that produce characteristic representations of maleness vis-à-vis women also create hierarchies and exclusions among men.

Within these alternative and suppressed masculinities there is or could be considerable overlap with the agenda of women's politics. These considerations necessitate a discussion of contrasting methodologies—those that render this sort of discursive construction both visible and problematic, and those that do not. Naturalism, reductionism, and essentialism are reviewed in a political as well as a theoretical frame, as there are important implications here for feminist politics.

Feminist debates have revealed considerable ambiguity in the way that *woman* is constructed as a category. I argue that a conception of men always and already informs these constructions, even if only implicitly. When men are there only implicitly or are given only cursory consideration, two strange things happen. One is that *woman* is defined rather narrowly as nonmale, that is, as *womb-having,* as a "difference that will not go away." This risks the reinscription of traditional femininity within contemporary feminism.

The other strange thing is that even when men are written into feminist theory in some ways, they suddenly disappear in others, although in everyday practice they are present, ubiquitous and powerful. Such issues include the characteristic "womb" issues of pregnancy (and by extension baby and child care), which are often conceptualized in an overly individualized and abstractly asocial way. Men's reproductive capacities and parental roles also tend to disappear in feminist theory, just as in traditional political theory these roles are generally forgotten. When they are noticed at all, they function in a symbolic way to help us forget that we forgot. Similar arguments apply to normalizations of masculinized competitiveness and marginalizations of violence that are characteristic of traditional political theory.

I conclude that the masculine/neutered subject is a misogynist political strategy that also serves to displace, disguise, forget, and merely symbolize a number of activities or potential activities, the invisibility of which serves the interests of dominant males. These activities include male sexuality and reproductive capacities, roles for men in child care and domestic labor, and sexualities men engage in that are alternative to dominant heterosexist masculinities. I argue for a concept of gender-critical theory that highlights the oppressive character of gendered practice, without capitulating to the simplistic narratives that construct the world of gender hierarchy and oppression in the first place (Grant 1989). In conclusion I suggest that finer-grained concepts based on agency and choice will have to be developed and utilized in order to theorize these issues in a politically productive way, as the traditional sex-gender-family trio will not do. Chapter 2 is thus devoted to a critique of a classic work on the family.

Engels's *The Origin of the Family, Private Property and the State* has attained great book status in political theory as an attempt to generate an overarching theory of economic and social development within the Marxist frame. But it has also become a classic of Marxist feminism, and of feminist thought generally, precisely because Engels formulated a theory of women's oppression in history. Despite numerous telling criticisms of method and detail, from all kinds of critics, the work is still widely read in tribute to its stated ambitions and its presumed feminist politics. In taking a perspective on men, I take a more critical view.

By examining Engels's famous theorization of reproduction as well as production through the ages, I present it as a narrative construction in which women and men are the major characters, playing out a drama governed not only by Marxist considerations of economic development but also by Darwinian presumptions concerning sexual behavior. In particular I argue that Engels's conceptualization of men is crucial to what he says about women, because once his presumptions about men are brought out into the open, his pronouncements on women look somewhat less in accord with the feminisms of his modern commentators. Moreover, his foregrounding of women in the narrative tends to disguise the role that men actually play in social change as he describes it, and this leads us to examine how sexual difference is handled in his text. Overall, he has produced an account of female oppression within an exculpatory narrative concerning men: in prehistory female oppression was caused by biology, but in historical times it is caused by class struggle.

The more aggressive aspects of dominant heterosexual masculinity are inscribed by Engels, first, into his conception of biological maleness and, second, into his conception of the bourgeoisie as class oppressors. Other aspects of conventional masculine behavior, chiefly the exploitative rather than the overtly aggressive dimensions, are never made problematic in his account. Hence they are validated as naturalized phenomena outside contemporary politics.

Engels makes the implausible claim that sexual oppression is first of all located biologically in sexual difference, but that sexual difference gives rise socially to class oppression. Moreover, he argues, again implausibly, that class warfare will solve the problem of women's oppression once the proletariat is victorious, because this will remove any motive for men to exploit women. Taking a "lifework" approach to Engels as himself a man, I discuss briefly the way that his behavior seems to have exemplified his theorizations of the sex war and the class war.

Engels's "personal" construction of male-female relations was obviously overwritten with conventional masculinist presuppositions, which is not surprising. What is surprising is the extent to which these presuppositions were themselves a function of class; Engels's relationships with women, and what he said within and about those relationships, differed remarkably according to the class of the female in question. This, again surprisingly, points to a dislocation between his professed class loyalty to the proletariat and his evidently bourgeois conception of social relationships. Following this lead, I look more carefully in Chapter 3 at how lives, which were once lived experience, are recovered for the great thinkers of political theory.

To do this, I examine the way that concepts in political theory are linked to biographies, and how this inevitably informs our reading. I make biography problematic by looking at the way that lives are constructed by biographers, and how meanings are derived by readers. Biography as a genre thus becomes problematic, and I discuss how I constructed one for Engels against the grain (Carver 1989). By that I mean that I made an effort to write in such a way that traditional narrative practices—birth-and-death framing, author-ial omniscience, teleological accounts, deterministic patterns, life beyond the grave, definitive closure on conclusions—are subverted. Indeed, the way that the biographer handles a great thinker as a biographical subject can lead to a curiously constructed overwrite of what was once the subject's real experience, namely a person's lifeworld before greatness was revealed by posterity. Thus, I argue that posterity often has too large a role in how biog-raphers handle characterization, as well as narrative time, which is mani-fested as printed space.

For that reason I choose, in my account, to let the subject's lifeworld, conceived as his formative years, dictate the arrangement of biographical space-time; and in pursuing that strategy, I deal in detail with Engels's per-sonal and private relationships. His domestic life, and the women who pop-ulated it, attain an unusual visibility, and this necessitates dealing with Engels "as a man," that is, both public man and private man, drawing atten-tion to the way that the supposed distinction does not work.

To do that, I place an overview of Engels's maturity in the central space of the biography. After that overview, I nest an account of his political activ-ities other than writing, and an examination of his great books and minor works, in two subsequent chapters. This has the effect of querying the usual procedure in intellectual biography, which is the reverse: great books, fol-lowed by political import, followed by personal life. It also has the advan-tage of querying the presumption that writing great books is doing great pol-itics.

I developed a reading of extant materials (mostly correspondence), in order to bring out the connection, albeit a limited one, between female emancipation as a contemporary issue and what Engels said and wrote (and occasionally drew, in the form of caricature) on the subject. The class-rid-den character of his references to female servants and the frankly bourgeois manner in which he conducted his love affairs (with working-class girls) are cited to show the complex ways that gender politics and class politics inter-act, often at cross-purposes. Within that frame, I draw attention to the way that friendship between men, such as that between Marx and Engels, gener-ated some of the most telling testimony concerning Engels's view of a par-ticular woman, Mary Burns, and his conception of himself as a man.

After this review of how and why I constructed my account of Engels's life, I shift the focus, in Chapter 4, from self-consciously constructed biog-raphy to a consideration of how the narrative traditions around our great thinkers of political theory arise in an almost untraceable fashion.

Contextualizing stories emerge and seem to accrete somewhat in the manner of process-without-a-subject. One of the prime reasons, so I argue, that we have the narratives we do is that they are good stories. What makes them good, in the sense of always holding our interest, is often their incongruity with what being a great thinker presumes—genius and authority. Foremost among these narratives in political theory is the one concerning "Marx's illegitimate son," and I follow the tale in a scholarly way, necessarily shifting from great thinker to great man. I highlight the discrepancy between what we know about the individuals involved in historical terms, and how they are made to perform as characters in a somewhat overheated narrative of scandal and shame.

The tale of Freddy Demuth emerges from a documentary source of uncertain provenance and consists in a juicy mixture of conventional genre and stock characterizations. It includes a surprise scholarly discovery, a long-lost letter, scandalous deathbed revelations, moral hypocrisy among the famous, a neglected child, an exploited serving woman, a wronged wife, a dutiful daughter, a long-suffering friend, and a faithful family retainer writing after the event to set the record straight. Biographers of Karl Marx, Engels, and Eleanor Marx have reacted variously in giving more or less credence to the document, to the tale as a whole or in part, to the veracity of the talebearer whether comprehensively or selectively, and to the claims that the story is of course essential, or alternatively irrelevant, to how Marx and Engels are treated as great thinkers and their works canonized as great books. This in turn bears on the way that feminist theory is conceptualized in relation to political theory. Thus, I survey how the story of Freddy Demuth has become part of the political theory tradition and of Marxist-feminist politics, and I conclude that the gender politics of the biographer or commentator has a considerable influence on the value assigned to the tale, to the way it is told, and to the conclusions that are drawn. About other political theorists, I might say, as Marx once did, *de te fabula narratur.*

In exploring the episode as one of gender politics, I give a rereading of the surviving documentation, meager as it is, that is actually contemporary with the lives of the principals, all of whom (save for Freddy Demuth) were dead by the time of the supposed narration. The complications of the class positions of those involved, and the different ways that gender politics was, or may have been, practiced within this family setting, constitute the major part of my discussion.

My conclusion is twofold. First, neither Marx nor Engels was the most likely candidate for the seduction of the housemaid (if such it was) and for Freddy's paternity (though someone was). Suspicion (if there need be any) should be directed toward any number of male émigré '48-ers. Second, quite considerable suspicion should be directed toward the documentary source, as the supposed narrator herself survived in a fit state to address posterity for another fifty-two years and seems not to have bothered to do so.

However, and more important, I draw attention to the way that narratives can layer themselves as characterization and then stick irrevocably as tradition. Sometimes this happens because they provide a personality for a great thinker that fits incongruously with the authorial majesty presumed to accompany a great book.

To explore further the use of gendered narratives in politics, I turn in Chapter 5 to the recent and highly publicized Clarence Thomas–Anita Hill hearings in the U.S. Senate, as reported in the New York *Times.* Besides its topicality, the episode is interesting because gender politics took the character it did, emerging within a context of class and race/ethnicity. These latter two discourses were themselves interdefined. The successful political strategy, so I argue, was one of narrative multiplication in which negative images and stereotypes were used to considerable effect. While neither Thomas nor Hill was (or is) an icon in political theory, they individually and together have a certain status in contemporary gender politics, and feminist politics in particular.

In analyzing this episode in U.S. politics, I make the conception of an event itself problematic by arguing that no analyst can use source material as a window within which an event can be framed and through which it can be viewed. Rather, all sources are not only selective—because there are no omniscient authors—but also there is no single event from which a selection could be made. All have their own versions of the hearings as a conceptual construct. Moreover, the boundary lines that are supposed to exist between participants, commentators, and observers are not actually there in practice. My apparently arbitrary limitation of source material to the *New York Times* for the relevant period reveals in that text itself how these distinctions are discursively constructed and unself-consciously subverted.

A theory of culture as a compendium of scripts allows me to level out race/ethnicity, class, sex, sexuality, and any number of other social factors as equally constructed through discourse and equally unnatural. This in turn leads to a considerable democratization in the way that individuals can be conceptualized as self-categorizing agents, but it also points to the myriad ways that disciplinary practices, often incorporated in stereotypes, can be used to frustrate and thwart the individual will. This provides me with a way to read the *Times* account as a record of the process in which narratives were deployed by all those quoted, and as itself a mobilization of metaphor in the language through which reporters constructed the texts I studied.

In the reportorial voices in the *Times,* events were portrayed as duels between Manichaean opposites, and the principal witnesses were adjudged truthful insofar as they were consistent. What counted as truths about the past, which could itself only be assembled and adjudged in the present, was also a question raised and never settled in the text. What was settled eventually was Thomas's nomination and the rejection of whatever cases, including Hill's, that might countermand the nomination. My conclusion is that Hill and Thomas themselves employed narrative strategies in self-conscious ways, and that Thomas's strategy of narrative multiplication was furthered by the ready availability in popular culture of negative stereotypes and unfavorable stories concerning women. Inconsistency in the very terms of narrative warfare was evidently no disadvantage, perhaps rather the reverse, as the incongruity value of sleaze seemed to be independent of, and inversely related to, the amount of contradiction there was between the various smears.

At the end of Chapter 5 I point to the closeness that must necessarily exist between popular culture and democratic communication between politician and voter. These discourses are examples of, or incorporate references to, a wide variety of genre in which valuations are framed. Any political activity that aims to move beyond a reinscription of the present must simultaneously relate to contemporary discursive culture and subvert it in an engaging way. While there is micropower seeping through ordinary relationships, there is also microreadjustment. It is from such almost invisible activities that new worlds unpredictably arise, and they need not revisit and reinforce the oppressions of the present.

My concluding chapter draws together what I have tried to do in political theory by arguing that gender is the ways that sex and sexuality become power relations in society, and not a synonym for women.

1

Feminist Theories of Politics and Postmodern Theories of Gender

Feminisms have put sexual politics permanently on the agenda of political theory. They have politicized sexuality, domestic labor, and reproductive and child care activities, and they have provoked a critique of naturalized conceptions of gender (Jones 1990; Jonásdottír 1991). They have caused turmoil in the world of supposedly fixed essences and identities by grappling with the difficulties of postmodernism and deconstruction (Ferguson 1991). The thesis that all phenomena in the human world are best understood as effects of linguistic constructions and performative behavior has profound implications for any theory of sexual difference, and feminists have not been slow to grasp the theoretical and political implications in highly controversial ways (Nicholson 1990).

At the same time, feminists have theorized individually embodied, historically contextualized subjects that live in a material world of experienced meanings. This interior narrative may be highly individualized, changing, and changeable; it may also be presumed and abstracted by political theorists seeking to generalize, and by activists seeking to politicize (Vance 1992). Feminists have exhorted theorists and activists alike to undertake the construction of a human subject only with due regard for sexual difference.

Feminists have provided the most challenging utilization of the Foucauldian perspective—that categories provide identities for individuals, which societies instantiate as oppression and constraint—hence the importance of their focus on women (Butler 1990). But there is still some distance to go in exploring this perspective on gender and the political issues that arise from it. Gender-critical analysis can open up political discussion of similarity and difference across the institutional and everyday boundaries of gender. Indeed, it is bound to make binary concepts of gender look multiple, and gender itself more permeable (see pp. 5–7). This will challenge some of the intellectual and practical justifications for conceptualizing certain issues as women's issues.

There are many reasons many feminists will find this kind of argument disagreeable (Grant 1993). However, it is my view that the long-term gains of stating and defending these views are considerable in terms of a potential for increasing freedom and equality. I also think that in the short term the masculinized world is much more at risk in this type of discussion than are feminisms as theorized and practiced by women.

My general aim in this chapter is to contribute to feminist theory by using postmodern theories of gender. This contribution is intended to be appreciative and constructive; the idea is to draw out substantive and methodological points concerning gender, in particular the way that maleness and masculinity/ies are represented and understood by particular feminists in recent works. My claim is not that men and masculinity/ies are misunderstood in these texts—far from it—but that the feminist discussions I cite identify a real contradiction, in theory as in life, that can be usefully explored.

Men's Theories

By focusing at the outset on a discussion of feminist writing, I am making myself vulnerable to a number of critical comments, about which I should like to provide immediate reassurance.

First, I am not writing to redress a balance or to defend men's rights or indeed men or maleness or any sort of masculinity/ies in any generic way. Perhaps there is something in these constructions that could be salvaged, but it is not my project here to attempt it.

There are perhaps some things that some men do best with some men, and I am struck with admiration for men who counsel violent men, visit prisons and try to talk to rapists; conversely I was not impressed with *Iron John* (Bly 1990) and the men's consciousness activities predicated on such views. Carrigan, Connell, and Lee (1985, 577) note with some venom that "when it comes to the crunch, the 'men's movement' is about *modernizing* hegemonic masculinity," helping "white, educated, heterosexual, affluent males . . . adapt to new circumstances without breaking down the social-structural arrangements that actually give them their power."

I take it that, after some decades of feminist politics, women's oppression is persuasively established, and the disastrous character of sexual hierarchy is equally evident. Men need help, but not because of women, and critical discourse about men in a feminist perspective can be distinguished, theoretically and politically, from men's movements.

Second, I would not wish to be associated with a view that only men can or should write about men; I am also hopeful that feminists would not be attracted by the "well, it's your problem" school of thought, as the problems are certainly everyone's. Men are noticed in feminist theorizing to a certain extent but drop out of sight quite quickly. For example, Riley (1988, 4) writes "a history of alterations in the collectivity of 'women,'" and asks,

"Why not 'men' too?" "The completion of the project," she says, "would demand that," and presciently she refers to "more radical work" that could be done "on the whole category of 'men'." Barrett (1992, 211) calls for "an understanding of men, masculinity and the interaction of the sexes," and refers to men as "the alternative rubric of 'gender'." But, disappointingly, the time to address the man question is displaced to the future. Coole (1994, 128 n. 2) also notes that "men and masculinity are indeed . . . implicated in feminist studies of gender and patriarchy," and remarks that "by no means all feminists are sympathetic to the development of men's studies." However, she does not detail the political and theoretical issues involved nor comment on feminists who advocate a more sustained centering of men and masculinity/ies.

As men are almost exclusive monopolists of positions of power and responsibility, I argue here that a constructive approach must focus on how this happens. Again, I am hopeful that feminists will reject the view that men are always and necessarily oppressors collectively and individually. Some conceptual space is surely necessary for things to change, otherwise they surely will not (Segal 1990).

Third, I am aware that there is excellent writing on men by women and that a feminist perspective includes this; I only wish there were more of these works (e.g., Cockburn 1983, 1988, 1991; Stiehm 1983, 1984; Elshtain 1986; Brown 1988; di Stefano 1991; Ferguson 1993). Indeed, the theoretical debates are particularly well focused in international relations, owing to the masculinized character of the discipline and the profession (I would mention Enloe 1990; Petersen 1992; Tickner 1992; Petersen and Runyan 1993). My particular aim is to bring together a feminist political critique, postmodern theorizations of gender, and, perhaps most distinctively, the sociological literature on men and masculinities.

Public Man: Feminist Critiques

In feminist critiques of contemporary political theory and political discourse, the human subject, as discursively constructed, is correctly identified as a man, and more specifically as public man (Elshtain 1981). Behind public man there is a private world to which woman is consigned through omission, tradition, nature, and explicit theorization. A considerable number of textual studies have convincingly shown this (Okin 1979; Lloyd 1984; Grimshaw 1986; Kennedy and Mendus 1987; Nye 1989; Gatens 1991; Coole 1993).

In the private world we find sexuality, domestic labor, and reproduction and child care, a realm of allegedly prepolitical or supposedly nonpolitical practices, presumptions, and structures, such as the family. The narrative

18 *Terrell Carver*

focus of classical theory and masculinized discourse is perforce on the public realm, where interests and concerns are supposedly very different; the
private is merely presupposed, protected, and regulated. The denizens of the
private—women, children, servants—do not appear in their own right in the
public realm. Indeed, man, who is none of these, has a role in public affairs
that keeps the other realm and its inhabitants where they belong. This feminist critique is neither uniformly presented in the literature nor uncontrover-
sial in detail, but the outlines are clear and convincing (see Pateman 1988
for a particularly lucid exposition).

Feminist theory has turned a critical spotlight on man, or the abstract
individual, as he appears in the classics of political theory and in contemporary political discourse, where the authorial "I" and "we" generally adum-
brate similar presumptions about the "us" of the audience. Man is variously
identified in feminist readings as patriarchal, misogynistic, dominatory,
materialistic, competitive, and violent (Spender 1982; Hartsock 1983;
Ferguson 1984; MacKinnon 1987; Connell 1987). He is said by many different writers to represent a male world, masculine values, or men's interests. Traditional political theory is generally said by feminists to be men's
theory; traditional history, men's history; and traditional politics, men's politics (Scott 1991).

Moreover, feminist theorists have argued that traditional conceptualizations do not just represent a masculinized world uncritically but also fail to
address other forms of plurality and difference, thus employing undue uni-
formity in presenting the human subject (Pateman and Brennan 1979).
Indeed, feminists have called for theorists to address racial or ethnic or class
differences, for example, much more explicitly in their writing (Bottomley,
Lepervanche, and Martin 1991). However, the feminist call for a theorization of differences has met with a response from a further quarter—namely
those interested in exploring differences among men, on the presumption
that these too are relevant to the theorization and practice of politics.

Feminism: Phillips and Mendus

To situate this development more precisely, I turn to two short works by
Anne Phillips (1992a) and Susan Mendus (1992), as I take them both to be
representative of widely respected feminist views in political theory (I shall
be drawing on other materials as well). Phillips and her co-editor, Barrett,
review the course of feminist theory since the 1970s. They sketch women's
disaffection from supposedly gender-neutral frameworks that covertly
exclude them from the public sphere; they rehearse the critical perspective
on women's oppression that was introduced within the practical politics of
race and class; they mention the ambiguities created by sexual difference

(i.e., androgyny vs. womanliness), and the subsequent postmodern turn in decentering the subject. They see the pitfalls of essentialism and of theory that universalizes in defiance of individuality (Barrett and Phillips 1992).

At that point in her discussion Phillips (1992a, 17–23) comments: "There is substantial agreement that conventional political thought has offered us men in a gender-free guise, and that all the talk of universal rights or citizenship or rules has taken one sex alone as its standard." "The question then arises," she says, moving from the theoretical to the practical, "how to correct for this bias towards men?" She reviews feminist theorizations of equality, justice, and representation, charting the tensions between an aspiration toward universality (in terms of some degendered or nongendered concept of the person) and a recognition of the fundamental importance of sexual difference in politics (interpreted as women's bodily experience of pregnancy and rape).

I do not think that I would quarrel at all with Phillips's conclusion (1992a, 27): that the way out of a repetitive dialectic of oppositions is "through comparison with those who are different, to reconceptualize what we had considered our essential characteristics as if they were accidents." But this is going to be difficult unless we are clear about how to conceptualize these differences in order to perceive them in a way that opens up the prospects for increased freedom and the reduction of oppression. For that reason, I think it is important to examine how maleness and masculinity are constructed by some feminist writers and then to contrast that with how those concepts are understood by writers in men's studies, and sociology of masculinity/ies, and by postmodern theorists of gender.

What I notice about the construction of maleness, bodily and otherwise, in both Phillips's and Mendus's writings, is a contradiction that evidently did not strike them or did not seem worth exploring. Phillips (1992a, 27) writes that "the very 'individual' of political discourse has been for so long a man," and that "orthodox notions of citizenship or equality have incorporated a masculine body." (I leave aside for the moment the possibility that a "masculine body" may not have to be biologically male.) Mendus (1992, 214–215) writes that democratic theory "in fact employs a male, rather than a gender-neutral standard," and that "in much traditional democratic theory the concepts of equality, difference, and disadvantage are themselves gender-biased: they assume a standard of normality which is inherently male." (I also leave aside for the moment the vexed question of the relationship between the concepts of sex and gender, and why it is that writers slip so easily into an ambiguous synonymy of the two.)

My claim is that the abstract individual or universal subject of political theory has been correctly identified by feminist theorists as male, but by theorists in men's studies and sociology of masculinities as, again correctly, "not a woman." This individual has also been correctly identified by feminists as degendered or neutered (Phillips 1992a, 27). Thus what is degendered is "not a woman," and what is male is "not a woman," either. Although it is true that both are "not a woman," what is degendered cannot be male, nor what is male, degendered.

Both Phillips and Mendus (and numerous others, e.g., Gatens 1991; Pateman 1988; Coole 1993; Kennedy and Mendus 1987) assume that the minimization of difference generally demanded in political theory is a reflection of a male world and male experience (Mendus 1992, 215–217). But the interesting question here is not whether there is any specifiable experience that is male, or if so, whether that experience is in some way more minimal than experience that is female (also supposing this exists), but rather *why* male theorists present their universal subject, which is so obviously masculine, as also degendered, a discursive strategy to which they closely adhere and to which feminist theorists have rightly drawn our attention. A discursive and performative account of gender, as given by certain postmodern writers, begins to resolve these contradictions theoretically by tracing out why the human subject was constructed in this contradictory way.

Studies of Masculinities

Intriguingly, modern sociological writing in what might be described as feminist-inspired men's studies (not the men's movement mentioned above) addresses this very issue, arguing that the abstract, normal, or stereotypical individual of theoretical and political discourse is certainly "not a woman" for reasons that are firmly established in women's history, feminist theory, and practical political contexts (Brod 1987). These reasons include the way that this subject occupies the public realm rather than a domestic one, the way it exemplifies an absence of pregnancy and other female bodily characteristics, and the way that it presumes a psychology of competitive self-interest in material things rather than a psychology of nurturing and a focus on emotions.

But is that enough to establish this individual as a man—biologically male, engaged with life in a male way, using or allowing masculinity to dominate women, experiencing masculine oppression meted out by other men, collectively constituting a male world? If one were simply arguing that men have problems that women do not, for biological reasons, or that men have experiences that women do not, for sociological reasons, then perhaps we could "add men and stir," as was once suggested with respect to women and social theory (Evans 1986). To some extent this is what men's studies and the sociology of masculinity/ies have attempted, particularly in the literature that focuses on men's life histories, lifestyles, and fantasies.

However, the problems inherent in this unexamined contradiction embedded in the subject that is simultaneously degendered and male are more serious than that.

Theorizations of differences among men have generally presumed a male-female boundary line, although some writers have taken great care to articulate their agreement with feminist views on differences of race/ethnicity, class, sexuality, and so on, among women and to support the overall claim that men are beneficiaries of women's subjugation (Brod 1987, 8–9; Hearn 1987, 13–15). Thus it is argued that masculinities must always be construed in the plural, and that concepts of men's differences must be constructed politically with respect to a feminist agenda. Much of the interest of the subject is therefore related to explorations of violence and to "masculinist" constructions of sexuality and other hierarchical relationships. Investigations into masculinities have historically been attuned to social class and other cultural differences among men, but increasingly, differences within the sexualities that are constructed for men, and within the ways that individual men experience them, have become a focus for investigation and theorization (Connell 1993a; Stevens 1993).

Thus, theorists in men's studies have argued that the human subject in academic discourse, such as traditional political theory and history, is certainly not a woman, but not therefore really a man, even as a useful abstraction. Their claim is that the generalizations and abstractions of theoretical discourse are untrue in politically relevant ways to the complexities of men's experience and to what is known of the social construction of masculinities. Feminist-inspired sociologists of masculinities have also concurred that this individual is not a woman but have suggested that inattention to the specifically female aspects of reproduction, and abstraction away from sexuality altogether, cannot count as an abstract representation of male experience, particularly the experiences that males have with dominant masculinities and with the alternative masculinities that some of them manage to construct (Carrigan, Connell, and Lee 1985; Connell 1987; Kimmel 1987; Brittan 1989; Morgan 1992; Hearn 1992; Brod and Kaufmann 1994).

While no abstraction can encompass all aspects of lived experience, there is nonetheless something wrong, in this view, in representing the human experience not just in terms that exclude important aspects of female experience and tend to evoke masculine experience as an archetype, but in ways that apply only to dominant and stereotypical forms of masculinity. Because dominant masculinities are taken to be archetypal by traditional modes of discourse, the struggles within which they are established are never presented, but rather forgotten or erased, and the abstraction *man* acquires an important disciplinary function vis-à-vis men as well as women. Actually, men are not born but made, and made in ways that are crucially relevant to feminist analysis.

Retheorizations of men and masculinities are various, though some academic theorists have sharply distinguished themselves from manifestations of antifeminist politics and popular therapies. The whole activity of retheorizing a positive identity within dominant masculinities, or indeed any masculinity at all, as historically constructed, has been dismissed as futile. A theory of liberation within the dominant subject position is necessarily problematic, in that the theoretical categories involved will always reinscribe the dualism *oppressor/oppressed*. The strategic symbolization of the oppressed as a category emblematic for humanity as a whole could hardly work for oppressors. Indeed, the attempted universalization of the categorial world of the oppressors is the object against which the emancipatory critique of such pseudoliberatory ideologies has developed (West 1989).

A call for men to cease being men has been issued, recalling Wittig's (1992) dictum that lesbians are not women. But it may be that any centering of men, however critical, and even within a feminist perspective, effectively decenters women as knowing subjects and as objects of knowledge. This will be raised as an issue below.

Methodology and Gender: Phillips and Mendus

An antiessentialist and antireductionist methodology, such as some feminists apply to women when they are attentive to differences within the category *woman,* could just as well apply to men (Brown 1987; Phelan 1989; Pringle and Watson 1992; Connell 1993b). Indeed, if this is attempted, the picture becomes interestingly complex. Having retheorized *woman* as a category incorporating differences—self-expressed differences among women—in the context of academic critique, and also in terms of political demands and activity, feminists have prepared the way, perhaps inadvertently, for a retheorization of men.

Methodologically, Phillips (1992a) argues an antiessentialist and antireductionist theoretical stance, and I take it that Mendus (1992) presumes this as well. This methodology rejects the naturalization of categories in terms of biology and bodies, or of social roles and structures. In the naturalistic view (which they criticize), individuals are normally constituted in a stable way (unless deviant or mentally ill); their behavior can then be described and explained as an effect of some cause. The rejection of naturalism means that one cannot read behavior or thought from biology, or determine what is functional or normal from a social system; ergo, wombs do not create women as maternal thinkers, nor does society need or create women as, at one extreme, homemakers or, at the other extreme, victims (Dietz 1992).

However, consensus on this antinaturalist methodology is not universal among feminists. Walby (1992, 48) refers (with disapproval) to "post-modernist arguments for the fragmentation of the concepts used in 'modernist' social theory" and to a consequent "tendency to shift the central theoretical concept away from 'structure' into 'discourse'." Perhaps courageously, she argues for the retention of the modernist project to "explain gender, ethnicity and class," and for the concept of woman in a bodily sense as "essential to grasp the gendered nature of the social world." How this theorization is to avoid the already well documented problems of essentialism and reductionism is not discussed, and the political point made in at least some versions of the postmodern project—that there is an element of self-definition, and variable self-definition, for individuals—is minimized (Butler 1990).

Theorizations of woman were decisively contested in U.S. feminism of the 1970s and 1980s by women (particularly those who were nonwhite, non-middle class, noncitizens of developed states) in the feminist movement, and a politics of negotiation among individual perspectives has resulted. The extent to which this is a praiseworthy empowerment or regrettable fragmentation is vigorously debated. But among at least some postmodernists, a theoretical stance based on dialog and contingency is now the norm, rather than the scientific conceptualizations grounded in notions of material causation and empirical validity, as apparently defended by Walby (1992; see also Nicholson 1990).

Although not (I think) postmodernists, Phillips and Mendus seem to me to have explicitly or implicitly rejected naturalism, that is, reductionism and essentialism, with respect to women. But while they have not restated the modernist project (which Walby [1992] does, unsatisfactorily), neither have they avoided a relapse into these methodological faults with respect to men, male, maleness, men's experience, or—a concept they do not use—masculinity (or, as in the better theorizations, masculinities). Their theorization of *male* gives an impression of something that is at least undifferentiated, and probably biological, as they barely allude to a definition. Maleness, in their arguments, is theorized explicitly as "unable to be pregnant and to give birth" and implicitly as something generally dominant and at times violent, viz. their references to public power, rape, and domestic violence. Femaleness is then defined, against this norm, as difference, and cogent arguments are produced as to why female experiences should be reconceptualized positively and not as "disadvantage, illness, problematic, other."

However, we are not given general characterizations of female experiences, but rather emblematic phenomena, assumed to be common and definitional. Neither Phillips nor Mendus explores femaleness as differences (plural), though they acknowledge that race, ethnicity, and class perspectives among women give rise to differences. Moreover, neither mentions sexual orientation, though a lesbian perspective in theory is well established.

Both go for a naturalistic version of "the difference that won't go away," viz. pregnancy, parturition, and lactation, though they do not put it quite like that, and both woman and femaleness in their work are really metaphors for these bodily phenomena. Perhaps *woman* tends to relate to reproduction, and *femaleness* to sexuality, though Phillips and Mendus are not much interested (in the chapters cited) in a systematic account that would helpfully distinguish the two (see Phillips 1992a, 23; Mendus 1992, 215).

The more individualistic, discourse-orientated, and interpretative strategy in postmodern theory—that different women interpret their bodily experiences differently, that they choose and control these experiences, that other experiences may be more important and influential, and that they sometimes for unavoidable reasons simply do not have these supposedly female experiences—does not significantly appear in Phillips's or Mendus's discussions. The recent feminist reinterpretation of science in general and of biology in particular, as pioneered in the mid-1980s by Haraway, does not get a mention, either.

Haraway (1991, 138) argues, quite imaginatively, that not only is femaleness a collection of various rather flexible conceptualizations of bodily and behavioral similarity and difference, but that the biology of sex and even of reproduction, far from being given in unambiguous physical terms, is itself an inscription of a gendered way of looking at the world. In this view there are an infinite variety of bodily differences that might be discovered, depending on the concepts (and politics) we employ to make discoveries. Science is a reading of the object, she explains, not a reflection of properties that are indubitably there. "Like race, sex is an 'imaginary' formation of the kind that produces reality, including bodies then perceived as prior to all construction." This suggests a politics of identification undertaken by a human agent, rather than identity politics given in a physical object, a politics of self-interpretation within and among culturally transmitted categorizations (Mouffe 1992, 235; Butler 1987, 133–134; Zerilli, 138–153).

In theoretical terms, some writing on masculinities (plural) is rather closer to the interpretative strategy at which some feminists have arrived, and somewhat more defensible for that reason. In that sort of writing, differences (plural) are presumed discursively, and elements of identity (not to mention behavior) are ascribed to individual agency. Individuals can thus reinterpret social categorizations in multifarious ways, and the constraints of socially enforced concepts like heterosexuality are also fully criticized, rather than left unexamined as natural. In short, a Foucauldian perspective is applied, and all the political problems of fragmentation that some writers have suspected or feared need to be dealt with. My point is not that the Foucauldian perspective in itself does this (notoriously it does not), but that the problems involved cannot be ignored, and that, crucially, when they are ignored some strange things start to happen.

Nonmales and No-males

One of these strange things is that *woman* is defined as *nonmale,* that is, womb-possessing (which paradoxically is the point from which a good deal of oppressive categorization begins), instead of more imaginatively in terms of what individuals actually choose, or attempt to choose, to do or not to do, or more intriguingly, to be, from time to time. From woman as nonmale, it might seem a short step to a resurrection of femininity as the way that such a cryptobiological category as woman is expressed, thus returning to a biology/behavior distinction that relates sex to gender. This has been thoroughly criticized (Pringle 1993). It may even be that some feminisms represent a new femininity, starting with the notion that having a womb is a "difference that won't go away," but the political relevance and theoretical defensibility of these views have been seriously questioned in an extensive literature.

Alternatively, there are politically and theoretically more astute conceptualizations of woman available. Ferguson's (1984) notion of woman as a category of oppression, one important category among many, actually works much better, in that the focus is on constraint and how constraint is mapped onto bodies. Thus, the relationship between womb having and political constraint is made contingent and arbitrary; other bodily differences could be (and are) identified as other and perforce as weakness, for just as little reason—for example, race or skin color. Womb having is not an essential weakness that justifies a protective feminism; rather, the view that weakness is essential, natural, and inevitable with respect to those having wombs is a view that lacks any compelling justification.

The lesbian and gay male perspectives become important here. What is post–women's liberation is also post–gay liberation (Carrigan, Connell, and Lee 1985, 583). The implicit heterosexism of the naturalistic narrative and of the "scientific" biological perspective gets decisively challenged when sexuality is cut loose from reproduction, or is at least reoriented. More disruptively, in the work of Butler (1987, 1990), the ironic, multilayered, highly individual, and self-defined character of gendered behavior appears on the scene, and most narratives of normality come to look like myths or symbols of themselves. This is because they deny their own multifariousness, even before they define a realm of otherness and deviance. This is to say that even straightness itself is underconceptualized in theory and overpoliced in practice. Butler's argument is that narratives or scripts of, for example, "normal heterosexuality" cover up the vast range of behavior in opposite-sex sexualities that actually occurs, and further, overassimilates it to reproduction and child rearing—themselves, of course, enormously variable in terms of personnel and practice.

Butler (1990) defines gender as a pattern of discourse that is characteristically binary and hierarchical, though not exclusively so, and mapped onto bodies as similarity/difference, desire/aversion. That is why there seem to be just two genders, male and female, and simultaneously to be many genders, such as lesbian butch and femme, effeminate nonhomosexual men, cross-dressing and transexuality, sadomasochism or various fetishisms, that are mapped onto bodies irrespective of genitalia (see pp. 5–7). That is also why, though lesbians are obviously women, Wittig (1992) can argue that actually they are not. Further, the whole notion of conceptualized practice itself, such as we see in a concept like gender, generates boundaries, which in turn generate transgressive behavior when individuals encounter and cross these supposed barriers—thus generating categorial dissonance and new categories (Butler 1990).

"Normal" heterosexuality, in this view, is not merely disciplinary but also fictional in character, in that challenges to it are rendered invisible or confusingly normalized in practice. A normality founded on deniability is thus maintained, and also on many occasions deviance meets with a blind eye. Butler (1990) comments that what seems to be important in terms of social discipline, thoroughly enforced as it is, is the reproduction of a symbolic code of normality and deviance, a code that is presumed to be central to the construction and regulation of acceptable behavior.

The other strange thing that starts to happen in some feminist theory is that men, having been self-consciously written into it (though at times in the degendered way that I have mentioned), suddenly disappear. This happens when some feminist discourse defines woman as nonmale, and female experience as that which men cannot have. Below I argue contrarily that all feminist issues, even womb issues, can be (some) men's issues as well, as (some) men are likely to be involved in them, one way or another, through presence or absence, by being supportive or dominating, in public or in private. It is also true in feminist analysis that these issues are not necessarily issues for all women, or at least not always issues of the same degree of salience or commitment for all women at all times.

Even if women lived together entirely without men and therefore (apparently) expunged any plausible claim that various issues were in any way men's issues, too, they would still face the well-known problem that gendered thinking poses: how to cope with these things in a way that is nonmale? Or in a way that is womanly or maternal? Or in a way that is not a reflection of masculinist thinking or values? Or reflective of a masculinized or instrumental approach to the world? Or an instantiation of masculinized science?

Dietz's (1992, 76–77) critique of "womanism" sums up the argument on terrain that is perhaps rather more relevant to feminism and political theory: "A truly democratic defence of citizenship cannot afford to launch its appeal from a position of gender opposition and women's superiority"; and "what this aim [of political feminism] requires is . . . a feminist determination to avoid 'womanism' while remaining attentive to women." Sex and sexuality, of course, are not the only guides to disadvantage, but unlike class, for instance, they are easily naturalized as physical phenomena and unhelpfully unified as cultural constants. Indeed, the gender script is written into the language we use, and it is very difficult to extricate oneself even linguistically, never mind in practice. By definition, this is a social rather than an individual matter.

Thus, a whole area of considerable interest vanishes when men disappear from women's issues. Men's reproductive capacities (about which they are notoriously reluctant to conceptualize in any constructive way) and parental possibilities (about which they are generally feeble and ambivalent) disappear entirely even as possible items for theorization and action, not to mention a role that men might have in the way that some women interpret sexual desire or a need for partnership or support. This happens, for example, in Mendus (1992) when she quotes MacKinnon on "men's physiology" and refers herself to "men's lifestyles." Notoriously, in MacKinnon's (1987) work, heterosexual desire is assimilated to men's violence toward and domination of women. Mendus merely links child care with mothering (paraphrasing de Beauvoir), rather than adding *fathering* or substituting the term *parenting*.

These are, of course, precisely the sorts of issues that recent literature in men's studies have highlighted, and not always in a sympathy-seeking and consciousness-raising way. The more challenging conceptualizations have examined gay-male parenting and campaigns to achieve parental or paternal leave, or to alter the balance between men's work inside and outside the home (Connell 1987). Self-evidently, the socially enforced and politically legislated career structure keeps gender divisions effectively in place; but it is gendered thinking that ascribes this to men's interests. The middle-class career structure and working-class wage structure are antiparent and antichild, and within these structures *woman* is deployed as a category of disadvantage, so that such child care as is accomplished in society is done as cheaply as possible, preferably unwaged. Child care is not in itself a disadvantage (our society makes it so); and there are no men's interests in any necessary sense (interests are socially constructed, and beneficiaries categorically assigned).

In short, if it is the issues that matter—pregnancy, abortion, rape, child care, misogyny, sexual self-expression—then "people" (Dietz's word) need to focus on which similarities and differences are relevant to those individuals involved, and which similarities and differences are not relevant, and theorists should locate themselves in relation to their own critical theorizations. The power relations involved when scientists or intellectuals find problems in the social world and thus make others objects of study and policy are now well known. Some of the women's issues mentioned above are also children's issues, for instance, but a child's perspective is not often addressed.

Public Man Again: Two Critiques

Thus, if both critiques—feminist and sociology of masculinities—of the abstract individual of political theory are right, as I think they are, the traditional human subject in political theory was never "she," nor ever really "he" in a sufficiently nuanced sense. This point became strikingly evident within the feminist critique itself. The disjunction between males and the dominant masculinities identified in men's studies was already visible within the feminist critique of public man, in that the invisibility of male roles (or nonroles) in reproduction, domesticity, and sexuality in social theory was exposed, and the violent, irresponsible, and oppressive character of dominant masculinities became visible when women were centered as subject and object in feminist studies. My claim here is that the strategic deployment of a particular kind of masculine subject in political theory has theoretical and political consequences that are only now being explored. The notions of displacement, disguise, absence, and symbolism are utilized below in order to deepen the critique of public man.

The most striking ambiguity in public man, as he appears in political theory and as he is explicated in the feminist critique, is that he is both male and degendered. This is also mentioned in Hearn's (1992, 3) critique of men when he comments that "generic universal Man [appears as] both neutral (neutered?) humanity . . . and as 'male'."

In the first instance, as we have seen, this man has a masculine body and is inherently male. Maleness here is theorized negatively as not displaying female bodily characteristics. But masculinity is also theorized positively as a psychology of competitive self-interest in material things, rather than a focus on nurturing and emotion.

However, in the second instance, this subject is paradoxically identified as degendered or neutered (Phillips 1992a, 27; Mendus 1992, 214–215). In political theory, as we know, the generic human is traditionally presented as unsexed, because sex is generally backgrounded as irrelevant. But when sex is made relevant, it is clearly a subordinate element in the way that human identity is conceived, viz. mapped onto woman (Brown 1987).

Feminist critiques have identified this representation of the human subject as implicitly male although explicitly desexed. The paradox is in traditional political theory, and feminist critiques have brought it out into the open, though not explored fully its implications. This has been my argument so far. What further conclusions can be drawn?

The abstract individual appears degendered because it is in the public realm. This realm is defined in opposition to the private precisely through a particular kind of abstraction, an abstraction away from sexual activity and reproductive attributes altogether. However, this is not to say that actual practice always respects this (Butler 1993). Thus, the abstract individual exemplifies an absence of pregnancy and other female bodily characteristics that arguably play a major role for females in self- and social-identity formation, and in the formation of political interests, whereas in political theory the individual that emerges is monotonically singular, unreproductive, and apparently sexless. Moreover, this individual is sometimes theorized as a rational consciousness in a way that suggests disembodiment altogether, as the body never really appears except as a presumed material substratum. The body is certainly not the site of the dramas of female corporeal existence, nor indeed of sexual reproduction or of sexual activity that need concern us, the presumed audience.

The extent to which violence to and by the body is taken seriously in traditional political theory is also open to question. While political theorists have a theorization of "force without right" (Locke), and "harm" in an evidently physical sense (J. S. Mill), in both the national and international public realms, overall, there is a feeling of safety within these narratives, or at least the creation of safe havens. This is reinforced in the public/private distinction, where the private is a realm of a particular security such that violence in that supposed sphere is so effectively distanced that it never figures at all. To a great extent in traditional political theory, violence is displaced in the narrative onto international borders, which are conceptualized as distant from domestic concerns (which in the experiential world they most emphatically are not), or more properly dealt with by international relations specialists, where Hobbesian assumptions of opposing interests have been the norm. Wars and conflicts have been conceptualized as out of the normal political realm. Violence within society is generally characterized as a tempting but minority activity, conceptually distant from the reasoned consent and dispassionate self-restraint exercised by citizen-subjects in the public sphere.

By virtue of the public-political/domestic-nonpolitical divide in traditional political theory, there is typically no theorization of domestic violence and continued threat. In "politick society," where, in Locke's (1988) words, "force is excluded," there are specialist agencies to deal with those who sacrifice the rights that citizenship bestows when they employ the violence that the law proscribes. But the violence these agencies have in mind is public, because the private is where harm does not occur, or when it does, the context is perforce transformed into the public realm.

The public/private distinction in political theory is thus movable with respect to harm and violence and the prevention thereof. As the state itself defines where the private is, and as even the liberal state has become

increasingly intrusive, the utility of the distinction in defending any spaces
or activities as purely private has been challenged, preeminently in analyses
of the gendered spaces and hierarchical sexualities that characterize stereotypical liberal ideas of domesticity (Locke 1988, 281, 415; Mill 1989,
80–115; Connell 1990; Evans 1993; Squires 1994).

The human subject of traditional political theory thus emerges as a disembodied nonwoman inhabiting a world that it makes safe for competing
adult monads (Arblaster 1984). Feminist critiques have drawn out the connections between war, masculinity/ies, and citizenship that lie beneath the
surface reassurances of the text and its unspoken presumptions (Stiehm
1983; Pateman and Gross 1986; Elshtain 1987). But why should the textual
representations of the human subject in traditional political theory have been
constructed in this paradoxical and ambiguous way in the first place?

The presentation of what is dominantly masculine as degendered or
neutered can be understood as a misogynist political strategy pursued within the founding narratives of political theory. This is a perspective "which
hides behind a mask of gender neutrality in order to subordinate women"
(Bock and James 1992, 6). It pushes sexuality, domestic labor, reproduction,
and child care into a private sphere and makes them women's work—except
when this sphere requires public regulation, in which case public man does
the job and what was private becomes the public realm (Walby 1990).
Indeed, theorizing this subject as disembodied altogether seems to negate
the need for any serious theory of the body and any challenging account of
bodily violence, most especially of male violence toward women, at home
and on the street or indeed anywhere else.

Thus, in political theory various characteristics of dominant masculinities are smuggled into the supposedly degendered abstract individual as normal or natural behavior through an imputed psychology of rational individ-
ualism. These theorizations have also been shown to slip into revealing or
admitting that this supposedly degendered subject is in fact male in reproductive terms, rather than female, and masculine in dominant modes, rather
than feminine. Gender neutrality and dominant masculinity are both
affirmed and denied for a reason.

Besides the relegation of sexuality, reproduction, child care, and domestic labor into the realm of private woman, there is this further result: Male
sexualities and reproductive capacities are also pushed into the background,
as well as a male role in child care and domestic labor (Bacchi 1991). These
are issues that have not been on the theoretical and political agenda as it has
come down to us in traditional politics, for public (or indeed much private)
discussion. Indeed, the point of these theorizations, in feminist analysis, was
precisely to structure and direct the definition of politics, and the course of
debate, in this way in the first place. A theorization of the family or of generation (i.e., reproduction) occasionally appears in the classic narratives,

albeit peripherally and contradictorily (Coole 1993; Gatens 1992; Pateman 1988). Arguably, theorists and politicians themselves are not anxious to give to men's differences from women even the limited attention that they give to women's differences from men. This is because sustained attention to these matters could well disturb the power relations that contemporary narratives of gender—including strategic silences—actually construct.

Thus, what might be problematic about men in terms of sexual behavior, reproductive responsibilities, and domestic and child care obligations is displaced into a realm where negotiated discussion need not take place. These matters have been conveniently relegated to the feminist agenda, on the presumption that feminists may discuss them powerlessly among themselves. Over many years, feminist theory has identified precisely those areas of male activity as sites where men victimize women, and feminist research has given voice to women's experiences of men. Moreover, theorizations of gay sexualities are beginning to trace the political subordination that gay men experience in relation to dominant heterosexist masculinities. This is the point at which a critical retheorization of men should begin, and this means that the gender-neutral but archetypically masculinized subject of political theory can no longer be unreflectively deployed. It is not a "merely conceptual" construction but rather an artifact of power struggles that we are supposed to forget, or never even to see.

The degendered and disembodied male is thus a disguise. It covers an absence. This absence is the void, in traditional political theory and in traditional political discourse more broadly, of theorization concerning male sexuality, reproductive capacities, and domestic roles in child care and other caring activities; or rather near void. Paternity is sometimes deployed in political theory, and in politics, as a symbol, chiefly of men as founders of republics or "nursing fathers," or as family men acting as heads of household in a paternalist manner, ruling over dependents (see, e.g., Locke 1988, 330–349). But there is very little interest in political theory, and in political discourse generally, in exploring those symbolizations in any detail in order to attempt to test their validity as abstractions from actual practice (Wolff 1978 is a rare exception). This is because it might well be discovered that in general men are not engaged in these activities in the way that the symbolization implies (Brown 1988, 205; Segal 1990; Seidler 1991a, 1991b). Fatherhood is mentioned strategically but forgotten theoretically. This serves to protect a position of privilege by making critical discussion unthinkable.

The abstract individual, besides disguising male sexuality, reproductive capacities, and domestic roles (actual and potential) with respect to women and children, also disguises the competitive and hierarchical character of dominant masculinities themselves with respect to men who do not exemplify them. Thus, other masculinities, particularly nonheterosexual and non-competitive ones, do not become visible theoretically or politically, because to make them visible would challenge the presumed inevitability in male development on which a supposed universal masculinity relies (Hearn and Morgan 1990). Indeed, the constructed nature of dominance is made to disappear in a naturalized manhood that purportedly explains and yet self-contradictorily necessitates the socializing of males into dominant masculinities, the policing of those who do not conform, and the exclusion of women in the gendered institutions of society. Perhaps socialization is best understood here as Hobbesian "dissociation," also remembering that men "make themselves Masters of other mens *[sic]* persons, wives, children and cattell" (Hobbes 1991, 88). As a term, *society* itself seems to suggest that struggle has ceased, whereas self-evidently there is a "more or less veiled civil war" (Marx and Engels 1980, 45).

Man and Woman

No doubt all men benefit from the naturalization and normalization of this masculinity vis-à-vis women, and conversely those women who can pass also do well out of it (Pateman/Hirschmann 1992). "Equal opportunities" moves this process along (Connell 1990). But not all men do equally well out of dominant masculinity, as it typically instantiates competition as well as self-interest, and by definition there are losers among men. Hence, theorizations that proceed from the abstract individual oppress and disadvantage women and some men (Hearn 1987). They also generate theories that validate class as historically inevitable and socially advantageous, even though the opening premise of equality might suggest otherwise.

Identifying the degendered nonwoman as a man or male misconceives the multifarious ways that dominant masculinity oppresses and curiously plays into the competitive conceptual structure by identifying all men as winners. Breaking out of gendered thinking, by thinking critically about gender, would tend to support behavior that was in effect nonmasculine, without therefore flagging it as feminine. This might be politically useful.

Woman as a category of oppression needs reversing; and, for feminist politics that aims to secure more positions of power for women, working from the category woman has been and should continue to be successful (Phillips 1992b, 78; Jones 1993). Any defensible political theory ought therefore to allow for group- and self-identification, and equal opportunities to promote the visibility and power of excluded groups (Phillips 1991; Young 1990). However, it is also true that women themselves differ over why, how, and where they ought to be visible, and what they might do with such power as they are able to gain individually. Thus, what constitutes an opportunity, and what equal ones might be, are both up for grabs in theory and in practice (Bacchi 1991).

However, it does not follow that these issues are best conceptualized in terms of woman, as a trade-off develops between relative ease of organization and unnecessary or counterproductive exclusions. Organizing directly on the sex boundary risks reinforcing the function of gender as a catchall source of categorizations and distinctions, and in particular risks reinforcing the particular way that these categorizations and distinctions are popularly understood today. Organizing around woman does not necessarily put child care on the agenda, or necessarily put it on the agenda in a way that is child-centered or even woman-centered. As has been noted, there is a risk that making something a women's issue seems to make it something that women naturally or necessarily do and men do not. Resourcing then appears as some kind of compensation for disadvantage, the very thing that Mendus (1992, 212–214) and others want to avoid.

A justification of state funding and support from the child's point of view would be refreshing; and it is certainly not the case that child care should have to be organized around women or even parents, heterosexuals, or young adults. "People who are adult and good at looking after children" might do; and children could be awarded resources (and rights?) as citizens. Perhaps the concept of political subject could be stretched to include them in meaningful ways.

Similarly, and perhaps more radically, it is not clear that rape is a women's issue, as it is men that do it, and some men that suffer it. Indeed, the complicity between masculinity and criminality is a large issue that people have an interest in exploring in a highly critical and, one hopes, transformative way. The pitfalls of woman as victim have been rehearsed; but the way forward is surely through some imaginative conceptualizations from which a politics could be generated. We are all vulnerable, one way or another, men included; again, feminist thinking has sometimes curiously flattered men into imagining that they conform to a "Terminator" ideal of masculinity. But it is more than likely that gendered behavior contributes to violent forms of masculinity that make women, children, and some men into victims. This is not to say that anyone needs any less attention as a rape victim than she or he is currently getting, or that women may need attention that men do not, or vice versa; rather that victims are not all of the problem, and that organizing the problem around women leaves the real problem (the rapist, and a masculinity of rape) caricatured or marginalized.

Similar points could be made about pregnancy. If it were not assimilated to the category *woman,* it could be evaluated as an activity in which men are necessarily involved at certain levels, and but contingently at others. The connection between woman and "someone caring for an infant" is also in need of complex theorization. Mother's milk need not be from a child's own mother, and it need not be offered by a female. Not all women are, can be, or want to be pregnant; not all carers for newly delivered infants are mothers or even necessarily female. Feminist politics faces the same problems in justifying, to many women who are not or will never be pregnant, special treatment for expectant mothers as it does in putting this issue to men, all of whom will never be pregnant (at least within present technology).

On the other hand, expectant mothers may very well have partners or friends who support them and their cause who need not be women. Pregnancy is not merely an individual event; it is an event in the lives of people other than the person experiencing the pregnancy, as inevitably others are involved. Indeed, it is argued that others acting as carers have needs to do with pregnancy, though they are not themselves pregnant. Defining pregnancy as a woman's issue is curiously body-centered and individualistic in a way that makes it difficult to conceptualize the other persons, and the various relationships, that constitute it as a social, that is, interpersonal phenomenon. Bodily experiences are individually interpreted by oneself, interpreted in a social context by others, and in a policy context by the state. In short, bodily experiences are highly public.

Practice and Theory

If the feminist perspective must be confined to women, and feminist politics to women's issues, then Braidotti (1987) and Modleski (1991) are right to argue that a focus on men in feminist terms, or participation by men in feminist activism, negates feminism altogether. Contrarily I would suggest that people (not necessarily all of them adult) will have to learn to cope with the realm of often unpredictable and indeterminate differences that commonsense discourse and particular dialogs reveal, and that gender is one of the least helpful ways now of doing this. This is because conceptually gender is a morass of naturalistic presumptions, confusingly various referents, slyly seductive euphemism, and politically potent symbolism. Because it constructs sexual (and usually reproductive) difference and maps it onto bodies, gender creates illusions of inevitability. These include the fictions that social life and personal identity are irrevocably organized around fecundity and potency (age, if nothing else, plays a role), and irreversibly inscribed in one's body (which is obviously not true, given genetic variation, individual choice, and reconstructive surgery). Our perceptions of gender are constantly reinforced and occasionally disturbed by the way that dress codes and narrative scripts are used by individuals to communicate, though the messages they send are hardly unambiguous: irony, parody, and uncertainty are characteristically part of the performance. Some of these performances are, of course, routinely raided and otherwise policed.

It hardly follows from this, as Walby (1992, 30–33, 48–49) suggests, that a perception of the dominatory force and disciplinary power of concepts such as man and woman need disappear from theory. Rather, it seems to me that the discursive theory of gender outlined above is a prerequisite to seeing how these categories are constructed—sometimes paradoxically—in the first place, and how speciously and destructively, on most occasions, they function. Pringle and Watson (1992, 68–69) say helpfully, "It seems clear that feminism can no longer ground itself in an essentialist conception of 'woman' or on an understanding of a 'gender identity' or 'interest' shared by all women." "If 'women's interests' are constructed rather than pre-given, so are men's," they continue, arguing that "if we have to let go of the authentic female subject, then we can let go too of the male subject." Politically, "this opens up the possibilities of exposing differences between men and, where appropriate, creating alliances," and it suggests a politics based not on unity, but on "respect for the differences of others, and on alliances with them." Pessimistically, though, Pringle and Watson warn against underplaying gender inequality in contemporary society and capitulating in an unthinking way to phallocentrism in discourse.

I have tried to suggest that traditional political theory is not so much phallocentric, phallocratic, androcentric, patriarchal, or masculinist as non-womb-oriented (whereas feminist discourse is); that traditional political discourse is also non-child-oriented (feminist discourse is not necessarily all that much more perceptive than men's studies); and that traditional political discourse is furthermore non-a-lot-of-other-quite-important-things-to-quite-a-lot-of-other-people-oriented. These are things on which quite a lot of other people quite possibly do have a discourse to which others ought to listen, political theorists in particular.

If traditional political discourse were really phallocentric or phallocratic, it would either be, or be more like, commonplace pornographic narratives, both textual and pictorial; MacKinnon (1987) employs exactly this strategy in reading phallocentricity into numerous forms of domination in society. Radical feminism of that sort has been criticized as obscuring rather than clarifying issues, and it represents another instance of gendered inscription as described above. Curiously, the view that the male (but as I argue, really nonfemale) norm is phallocentric reflects uncritically the commonplace kind of masculinity that equates identity with "dick," just the sort of synecdoche that a sociology of masculinities is seeking to undermine.

Conclusion

My point in this chapter is to argue that people need to find identities (plural) other than ones that are centered on bodily organs, that they ought to be imaginative and empathetic about doing so, and that gendered discourse is highly suspect as a way of helping them along. More radically, the concept *woman* holds its *differences* together only so long as man or male is constructed as a monotonic other without differences or history (Kimmel 1987; Brod and Kauffman 1994). Feminists who view their movement as one "to liberate people from gender," because gender is a source of unnecessary constraint, seem to me to be on the right track (Grant 1989, 8; Haraway 1991, 148). I would argue that a distinction could be developed between the gendered nature of the social world grasped in a gendered way and the gendered nature of the social world grasped in a way that is critical of gender itself. The latter might be termed gender-critical theory. It would highlight the oppressive character of gendered practice, without capitulating to the universalizing and naturalizing narratives that construct the gendered world and insulate it from political challenge.

This is not to say that anyone has any particular rights, duties, or obligations that follow in any simple way from any given conceptualization; rather, that some conceptualization of the interpersonal character of this supposedly personal experience needs to be carefully undertaken. *Family* is a classic case of how not to do this, as it is a notoriously ambiguous and loaded term, confusing whom one is related to, whom one lives with, who does domestic tasks, and who looks after children, among other things (for a critique of one particularly famous attempt to theorize the family, see pp. 37–53).

Finer-grained concepts will have to emerge, partly from political debate and partly from theorists who seek to contribute. Deconstruction need not be destruction; clarity in thought could produce better politics. On this point I have tried to be more illustratively specific than Mouffe (1992, 235), who writes of "a problematic that conceives of the social agent not as a unitary subject but as the articulation of an ensemble of subject positions, constructed within specific discourses and always precariously and temporarily sutured at the intersection." Specificity can always be argued away, but at least we know what is under discussion.

Fighting gendered concept with gendered concept locks politics into a circle of despair and domination, as that is the nature of gendered concepts (Harding 1992, 352–353; Squires 1993). Merely putting a womb into the abstract individual will not in itself get us to the most useful retheorizations of politics. Gender as a category, and as a set of social scripts instantiated in practice, as individuals make it happen, needs critical examination in relation to any number of issues, probably all issues, given the way that gender as a catchall category influences our identities and cuts across our lives. Catchall categories, such as gender, sex, and woman, catch too much and too little. Theory is there to subvert this process, and in the next chapter I take on a famous theorization of the family.

2

Theorizing Men in Engels's
Origin of the Family

*In returning to the past I am talking of the present. I am interested in the past
to the extent that it speaks of the present. This is so both in the general sense
that speaking of the past is always speaking of the present, and in the specific sense that speaking of certain aspects or periods of the past speaks
directly of the dominant powers in the present . . . the powers of men.*

—Hearn 1992, 9

Family is an ambiguous concept, stitching together highly variable assumptions concerning women, men, children, and their relationships within and
outside such boundaries as define family in nuclear or extended form.
Moreover, the family is interdefined with concepts of sexuality, production,
and domesticity, such that it often stands in for the very assumptions through
which it is constructed. Theoretical works on the family have generated considerable debate, and these debates are ways of moving issues onto the political agenda and provoking change. Any view of what the family is, has been,
or might be necessarily relies on reference or allusion to classic narrations
of the constituent concepts. Given what I have argued in Chapter 1, it will
be worth revisiting one of the most influential accounts of modern times.

Engels's *Family*: In What Sense a Classic?

Friedrich Engels's *The Origin of the Family, Private Property and the State*
was first published in 1884, and since then he has been widely praised for
raising issues and opening debates. The work itself has become a feminist
classic (Sayers, Evans, and Redclift 1987). For some writers it is evidence
that feminists should reject Marxism, or even Marx's own work—which
Engels's book is not. But for others it is the foundation of a Marxist feminism—its deficiencies notwithstanding. Barrett (1983, 214) comments,
"Scarcely a Marxist-feminist text is produced that does not refer somewhere
to Engels's argument, and if one had to identify one major contribution to

feminism from Marxism it would have to be this text." As we will see below, the notion that Engels's argument is singular is highly problematic, but otherwise for present purposes the point is taken. Engels produced a classic.

Marxist-feminists have on the whole been generous to Engels, though there have also been numerous telling criticisms. Nonetheless, the general trend of approbation makes it difficult to see how deficient the work actually is. Few commentators, feminist or otherwise, would defend very much of the anthropological material Engels cites or very many of the anthropological points he makes independently. Barrett (1983, 214) rightly describes the text as "flawed and disputed." Many of the assumptions held by the nineteenth-century anthropologists to whom Engels refers, and many of those he held independently, are also rejected today, a rejection duly noted in the critical literature.

But the book's classic qualities lie elsewhere. Did not Engels raise issues of enduring importance about the sexes, the division of labor, and the development of political power? And in particular did he not overcome a commonplace sexism and make explicit the role of women in these affairs? For those reasons he has attracted feminist interest. Whether he should also attract feminist praise, even endorsement, is another question. Blurring critical interest with praise and endorsement, as I argue, generates vagueness and makes arguments difficult to sustain. The hagiographical frame, however qualified, must really be stripped away if any account is to be genuinely and usefully critical.

Some of what Engels says has attracted feminist amendment (Delmar 1977; Vogel 1983). But elements of his account have sometimes been allowed to stand because of what they evoke in the mind of the commentator. Thus the non sequitur and the quotation out of context make their appearance in the literature when Engels is credited with views he did not hold, and some of the views he did hold are brushed aside too quickly (Delmar 1977, 273, 287; Leacocke 1981, 41–44). In particular the status of hypothetical accounts of prehistory is not squarely faced in the various debates about whether Engels's contributions to this genre are good ones, or indeed whether the genre has any validity at all. His arguments about biology and natural selection as they affect his views on the physical and sexual oppression of women are not examined critically enough, since commentators are inclined to set his neo-Darwinian account of the family on one side while taking what he says about modern monogamy, which is generally quite negative, as read (Barrett 1985, 28–30). And most crucially of all, his assumptions about male behavior are not taken as seriously as they should be, because what he says about the economic oppression of women can be accurately grasped only in conjunction with what he says about the "opposite" sex. This is because it is the economic interaction between men and women that propels his account of past, contemporary, and future relations between them. There are two sexes involved, and it takes attention to both to render a critical reconstruction coherent.

My central claim here is that the work as a whole tells a story, and that piecemeal criticism misses the underlying point. Much of the significance of Engels's text, and of others like it, is recoverable only through narrative analysis (Scheppele 1989; Lavoie 1990). An important but little researched aspect of that story is that it is about men. In theorizing women, Engels also theorized men, and this is a theoretical nexus that needs investigation (Connell 1987; Hearn 1987; Brittan 1989; Segal 1990). My purpose here is to explore *The Origin of the Family* as an element in Engels's lifework, developing a critical account of how he theorized men and suggesting strategies for contemporary theory and politics.

Engels and Sexuality

The historical approach to sexuality was as unpopular in conservative quarters in the 1880s as it had been in the 1840s when the *Manifesto of the Communist Party,* written by Engels and Marx, was published. Indeed, it is surprising even now how naturalistically rather than historically sexuality is conceived, despite the appearance of influential, even landmark works in history and sociology (Foucault 1984–1988). Engels deserves some minimal praise for continuing, in *The Origin of the Family,* the critique of "the bourgeois family" begun in the earlier joint work of 1848 with Marx, and promoting inquiry into areas that were presumed to be natural or private, according to the assumptions of his time and ours. *The Origin of the Family* was the first work in the Marxist tradition explicitly to address the woman question, though admittedly this was to some extent a matter of the word *family* in the title; in the *Manifesto* "bourgeois clap-trap about the family" and communist plans to change "the status of women" also received attention, though the treatment was notably negative, detailing what was wrong but saying little about how to put it right (Marx and Engels 1980, 49–50, 449–583).

Engels claimed to have used Marx's notebooks when he wrote *The Origin of the Family.* This is probably true in a superficial sense, Marx having died in 1883, but Engels's substantive claim that he reflected Marx's views has been carefully scrutinized in terms of content and found wanting (Krader 1972; Carver 1983, 144–145). The historical and anthropological account in the text is very much Engels's own.

The status of Engels's writing as history or anthropology is somewhat misleading anyway; it is much more like a historical novel—Galsworthy's *Forsyte Saga* comes continually to mind. Formally, Engels aimed to survey the entire history of sexuality, reproduction of the species, and production of goods and services in all societies, however primitive, in order to produce a history of political forms leading up to the modern bourgeois state. In common with other nineteenth-century accounts, his approach involved the demarcation of historical stages, causal explanations for change, and an assumption of progress in the development of civilization. As a Marxist, he foresaw the resolution of the conflicts he detailed through the eventual victory of the proletariat over their class oppressors.

But unusually in his own time, Engels considered women to be further oppressed and moreover argued that this oppression was the historical product of a fundamental change in human relationships. Startlingly, he claimed that the imposition of male domination over women made women the first oppressed class. (Conceptual connections between gender and class are explored in Chapters 4 and 5 below). As a historical product, this oppression was judged by him to be remediable and transitory. Thus, the story Engels told is ostensibly about changes in the relation of one sex to another, with a promise of further change as the class struggle develops. It is a complicated account that I will examine in detail.

Part of my interest here is to trace the twists and turns of the plot, as Engels constructs it, men and women being his main characters. But another reason the text is interesting is that it prompts us to reflect on the consequences of foregrounding women as narrative subject and analytical object. Men appear in Engels's account only secondarily, in contrast to his focus on the oppression of women, yet, for Engels, women's oppression is inexplicable without men. He clearly found that he need say little about men in order to make his narrative work; he employed assumptions about men that were so obviously simple and "factual" that they required little explanation. Women, of course, were more problematic for him, and doubtless in his view for readers as well. His narrative is thus preoccupied more with material concerning women than with a discussion of men, who were, after all, the agents of domination. This has the effect of covertly reproducing conventional men's history, that is, history written on masculinized assumptions, while appearing to be a history focused on women.

Engels's theorizing about women proceeds against a background of unexamined assumptions concerning men, and the fact that he made women problematic obscures the fact that he treated men unproblematically. His story is actually driven by men, but they appear somewhat marginally and mechanically in the narrative. Through this discursive strategy, Engels prefigured contemporary feminist narratives and theorizations, and in this way reproduced an important political weakness, namely a lack of detailed engagement with men and masculinity/ies. It is time now to bring men in, but in an appropriately critical framework (Morgan 1981).

Engels was not simply an unwitting victim of traditional assumptions

and values; rather, his narrative was itself a traditional exculpation of conventional dominant masculinity. This masculinity was important to him
politically, as political action that did not validate those norms and conventions was virtually unthinkable; despite the superficial feminism of *The
Origin of the Family,* Engels never associated himself with women's struggles as women. To do so would have lost him such political allies as he had
and gained him little in the way of usable political clout.

Moreover, conventional masculinity was important to Engels personally, as episodes in his self-development and later relationships were constructed from characteristically masculine scripts. Examination of early letters and drawings reveals what might be termed "a secure gender identity"
that never rubbed against the class-based radicalism that he adopted early on
and adapted but little. Throughout life he was quite capable of sympathizing
with the oppressed and workers of the world, but then complaining vituper-
atively about his servants, who were always female (Carver 1989; Cockburn
1983; Butler 1990; see also Chapters 3 and 4 below). How then does *The
Origin of the Family* attempt to reconcile a view that women are peculiarly
oppressed by men with an unexamined and presumably naturalized masculinity that was conventional, even bourgeois?

Production and Reproduction

Engels made it his business to consider the condition of women in prehistory, in contemporary societies where technology was little developed, in the
history of recorded civilizations up to the present, and in the communist
society he envisaged for the postcapitalist future. He also amended the materialist conception of history—the theory he attributed to Marx and which he
himself espoused—to cover the stages of development of the family (Carver
1983). This he interpreted very loosely as both kinship arrangements dividing tribes into clans and the organization of households to include parents
and children.

According to Engels's materialist conception, the determining factor in
history in the last resort was the production and reproduction of human life.
He added an important gloss on production and reproduction, saying it was
of a twofold character: the production of the means of subsistence, including food, shelter, and tools; and the production of human beings themselves,
which takes place within what he variously termed "the family," "groups
based on ties of sex," and "the family system."

The family was further subject to natural selection and to the sexual
behavior that Engels thought was characteristically different in men and
women. Both kinds of production—labor on the one hand, procreation on

the other—were said to condition the social institutions of any given coun-
try during any given historical epoch. And conflicts traceable to production
and procreation were said to account for major historical change as one
epoch succeeded another (Engels 1980, 449–450).

It appears that Engels established two autonomous lines of explanation
for the social order: economic relations and family relations; the class war
and the sex war. But it is difficult to reconcile this theoretical preamble with
the story that he actually told, which informed us that the old society of prehistory was built on groups based on ties of sex, but domination of the social
order by those family relations was itself an appearance: "the less the development of labor, and the more limited its volume of production, and, therefore, the wealth of society, the more preponderatingly does the social order
appear to be dominated by ties of sex" (Engels 1980, 449–450).

While it is true that Engels referred to the old society as based or built
on those ties, his portrayal of historical change presented the family as dominant in society only when the alternative kind of production had not itself
developed beyond the merely rudimentary production of subsistence.
Historical change was not explained by development in the family system.
And the development, if such it was, in the ties of sex considered by Engels
was reactive, rather than autonomous. The old society burst asunder when
assaulted by newly developed social classes, whose members were not tied
by sex but by economic interests founded on productive labor, which the
property system reflected and enforced. The property system then came to
dominate the family system (Engels 1980, 449–450).

In the old society the production and distribution of subsistence goods
was ordered by sex and clan. In the new society relations between the sexes
and the rearing of children were entirely dominated by the property system,
class antagonisms, and class struggle. Thus, it is difficult to believe that
Engels took his theoretical dualism seriously when one factor (labor)
accounted for the most significant of all changes in the other (the family)
and not the reverse; when the most significant historical change was not
traced to one factor (the family) but explained by the other (labor); and when
the most significant instance (the old society) in which the family was said
to have had a determining role was declared to be one in which this only
appeared to be the case. Here we have an instance of taking up a position in
order to put it down again; this tactic is sometimes described as "noticing."
Tracing social change to reproductive labor would have epitomized labor as
female, particularly in the absence of any determinedly interpretative work
on men's actual or possible roles in "childwork." Engels was neither
equipped to do this—his liaisons produced no offspring—nor particularly
interested in such matters. His letters and papers reveal no special concern
with children or even family life in any practical way. In his discourse, family functioned only symbolically (Carver 1989, 133–171).

Sexual Selection

So far it is not clear that the categories *reproduction of human beings, ties of sex,* and *the family* are doing any work in Engels's analysis. But perhaps they might help in making sense of the sex war within the overall context of the class war that he discerned in history and documented in contemporary society in his *The Condition of the Working Class in England,* published in 1845. If so, this might temper any criticism that his outlook was not just Marxist but masculinist or simply male by virtue of the priority assigned to physical work outside the body and the exclusion of emotional and body-centered activities from analytical importance. This charge has been leveled at Marxist (and Marxian) theories of class struggle (Hearn 1987).

At this point the reader should also be warned of numerous questionable assumptions in the text beyond those amounting to a gendered characterization of labor. Some of the categories employed by Engels derive from the writings of Lewis Henry Morgan (*Ancient Society, or Researches in the Lines of Human Progress from Savagery, through Barbarism to Civilization,* 1877) and J. J. Bachofen (*Das Mutterrecht,* 1861); and some derive from Marx. The mixtures and modifications, of course, were uniquely Engels's.

Engels assumed that all civilized peoples have a structure of kinship terms and marital patterns that developed through distinct, necessary stages from a common, original form. Moreover, he assumed that the practice of currently existing but technologically primitive societies provides evidence that unobserved stages in the development of the kinship and marital structures of civilized peoples existed in the expected stages. And he assumed that unobserved, primitive stages of marital patterns can be deduced from the language of primitive peoples when their kinship terms appear to conflict with their actual marital practices (Engels 1980, 458–459, 466–480).

More crucially, Engels introduced assumptions about natural selection and sexual behavior. He assumed that natural selection was behind successive alterations in kinship restrictions on marital partners, and that sexual behavior in males differs from that in females in important respects. According to Engels, all marital and kinship structures developed from an original condition of promiscuous intercourse, to group marriage according to generations, to mutual community of husbands and wives within a definite family group, and then to what he termed the pairing family, which he then distinguished from modern monogamy. This proceeded as natural selection benefited those clans in which marriage among relatives was forbidden, first between near relations and then between remoter relations in an ever-widening circle of exclusion (Engels 1980, 474, 484–485).

The result of this development was that men, whom Engels assumed are the sexual predators, were denied access to more and more women, so it was men who began to obtain partners by abduction and purchase. Thus, within the pairing family and modern monogamy, Engels claimed, polygamy and infidelity remained men's privileges, while men demanded strict fidelity from their wives and cruelly punished adultery when it occurred during the period of cohabitation. He assumed further that the sexual nature of women was such that once the promiscuous sexual relations of the jungle had lost their "naive" character, women found a pattern of promiscuity degrading and oppressive. He suggested that they longed for chastity and saw the right to temporary or permanent marriage with just one man as a deliverance. Thus, he cast them as the opposite of sexual predators, as the partner sought rather than the one who seeks, without giving reasons for this characterization (Engels 1980, 484–485).

Women are credited by Engels with the advance away from promiscuous behavior toward monogamy. But in his view they were tricked, since men contrived to oppress them. This happened when men were unfaithful and deprived women of the stable relationships that Engels assumed they desired. How men could find adulterous women was not detailed, since Engels's account was limited to his version of male motivation—the pleasure of multiple partners. Marital relations were therefore stable to the extent that men found further pursuit of sexual partners a distraction from the time they could spend having sex with the one they already had. Needless to say, the presumed imbalance in intellectual power or moral character between men (who were clever but devious) and women (who were good but naive) was not explored either (Engels 1980, 485).

Engels (1980, 502) assumed that the three forms of marital relations he identified—group marriage, the pairing family, and stable monogamy—were developments characteristic of three stages of economic development—savagery, barbarism, and civilization. But the relationship between the forces of natural selection and sexual behavior (which supposedly accounted for the development from group marriage to the pairing family) and the economic development in stages from savagery to barbarism (by means of cattle breeding and agriculture) was not explored (Engels 1980, 461). Were those two factors (labor and procreation) linked? If so, how—and why? If not, which one explained which aspect of this complex transition?

The upper stage of barbarism attracted Engels's particular interest, because it was there that he looked for the origins of civilization. For Engels, civilization was ultimately the capitalist economy and its corresponding family form—modern monogamy and the nuclear household. Crucial to an understanding of Engels's position is his view that the pairing family (and the preceding forms of group marriage) were matrilineal. It was clear, he said, that descent was traceable only on the maternal side. The female line alone was recognized, since natural fathers cannot be determined with certainty. The exclusive recognition of a natural mother, he assumed, signified high esteem for women. Though the marriage tie in a pairing family might be easily dissolved by either party, the children would then belong solely to the mother. Within the household, the women would come wholly or mostly from one kinship group, which men then joined. Female children would remain, and male children would marry outside the household and matrilineal clan (Engels 1980, 484–488).

Moreover, Engels assumed that the primitive communistic household, within which group marriage and the pairing family were supposed to have functioned, implied the supremacy of women in the house, because they ruled the common stores, and men did the providing under female supervision. Women thus had a free and highly respected position among savages and barbarians (Engels 1980, 481, 484–488).

The overthrow of this mother-right must have come, Engels argued, with the development of new sources of wealth deriving from outside the home. The savage warrior and hunter had been content to occupy second place in a household where division of labor between men and women had regulated the distribution of property, giving superior rights and status to women. Herds and other new sources of surplus wealth turned this upside down, causing women's housework to lose significance compared with men's new efforts outside the domestic economy. Where wealth had once been contained within the female province—the house, clothing, ornaments, culinary implements including boats and weapons—the new economy won surplus goods through cattle rearing, metalwork, weaving, and tillage. Engels assumed this to be men's work and the goods to be men's goods. Moreover, he presumed that the results remained the man's property if he were required to leave, while the woman retained the fixed household possessions. The text is devoid of evidence justifying these presumed differences between women and men (Engels 1980, 485–488).

As men's wealth grew, so their status increased, and there arose a stimulus for them to overthrow matrilineal reckoning of kinship and inheritance. According to Engels, a divorced father would want his children (who must stay with their mother and matrilineal clan) to inherit his own goods and would accept no doubts about paternity, because with pairing marriage his paternity was more nearly certain. In consequence, men established the patriarchal family and then eventually modern monogamy, in which men declared themselves supreme. In Engels's view, modern monogamy included the hypocritical privilege of infidelity—for men only (Engels 1980, 485–488).

The overthrow of mother-right, Engels wrote, was the world-historic defeat of the female sex. It was also the victory of private property over common ownership. More strongly, he added, "the first class antagonism which appears in history coincides with the development of the antagonism between men and woman in monogamian marriage, and the first class oppression with that of the female sex by the male." How some men went on to oppress others as well through the economic system was then outlined, starting with slavery (Engels 1980, 494–495).

Sexual Relations and Property Relations

Before noting Engels's assumptions about bourgeois and proletarian monogamy, including the related and somewhat novelized matters of adultery, hetaerism, cuckoldry, prostitution, "boy-love," exclusive domination of the family by the husband, wifely rebellion, and women wearing the breeches, it is important to consider an assumption he made about the relationship between the division of labor (including the overall amount) and social status. Engels assumed that the division of labor between the two sexes was determined by causes entirely different from those that determine the status of women (and men?) in society. In the communistic household, where Engels assumed women were held in high esteem because of the matrilineal kinship system and because of their supervisory role in the necessarily domestic economy, women (in some cultures if not all) were burdened with excessive toil. This in no way conflicted, so he said, with high status and real respect for women in society. The lady of civilization, whom Engels said was estranged from real work, was surrounded by sham homage, making her infinitely lower socially than the hard-working woman of barbarism, who was regarded as a "real lady." The masculinist assumptions behind this gendered account of respect are of course not made explicit in the text (Engels 1980, 481–482, 568–571).

Engels assumed that civilized monogamy arose out of the concentration of wealth in the hands of one person—a man—and out of his desire to bequeath this wealth to his own children exclusively. Monogamy was the supremacy of the man over the woman, and the individual family was the economic unit of society. This was the first form of the family based on economic conditions, not on natural ones, since it represented for Engels the victory of private property over original, naturally developed common ownership. The new sources of wealth arose, so he assumed, out of productive activities organized within the framework of private property, which seems to have arisen out of an individualistic—and male—desire for each man to secure his own property for his natural children. Engels was himself somewhat nervous about the obvious anachronism here concerning "the man of property" (Engels 1980, 485–488).

Engels assumed that bourgeois marriage, as an institution, engendered hetaerism and prostitution as men hypocritically pursued a sexual freedom supposedly ruled out by monogamous marriage. When women, neglected by their husbands, took paramours, they were (once again) severely punished, and the domination—sexual, physical, and economic—of the bourgeois male over his household was assured (Engels 1980, 499–500). This was incompatible with Engels's view of romantic (hetero)sex(ual) love, which could become the rule only among the proletariat. There the economic foundations of monogamy were removed, because there was "a complete absence of all property" and therefore "no stimulus here whatever to assert male domination." Instead, personal and social relations different from those of a bourgeois marriage came into play, so he believed, particularly when large-scale industry transferred women from the house to the labor market and factory, and often made them the breadwinners of the family. Since many sexual unions were not legally sanctioned, and since proletarians lacked access to the law (which cost money), the woman regained the right of separation. Engels's conclusion was that male domination disappears— except, perhaps, for some of that brutality toward women that became firmly rooted, so he assumed, with the establishment of modern monogamy (Engels 1980, 499–500).

This passage throws an interesting light on Engels's successive sexual relationships with the proletarian Burns sisters, Mary and Lizzie, whom he supported in Manchester in a household separate from his bachelor quarters. Mary died in 1863; unusually, there are no surviving photographs of her and practically nothing is known about their relationship. On her death Engels berated Marx by letter for insufficient condolences concerning the loss, yet it is possible that the evidently embarrassed Marx had actually read the situation well enough in his first, rather offhand reactions: it had not struck him that Engels cared so deeply (see pp. 72–73). Though Engels later lived with Lizzie in London after his retirement from business in 1869, and while in residence with him she kept house, he did not marry her until she was on her deathbed in 1878. Was Engels when a bachelor defiantly flouting the conventions of bourgeois morality by living with an unmarried woman (Barrett 1983)? Or was he not conforming all too typically to another bourgeois convention, whereby discrete liaisons and housekeeping arrangements with socially inferior women were preferable to marriage across the forbidden boundary of class? A working-class Frau Engels would certainly have been unpleasing to the bourgeois family in Germany to which Engels belonged, and whose property was partly in his charge while he was alive and an obvious item in his will should he predecease a spouse (Carver 1989, 145–161).

Perhaps Engels's relationships led him to the conclusions detailed above concerning the domestic life of proletarians. But I think it more likely that his romanticized views were ones that his privileged circumstances allowed him to hold. They also conveniently distanced him personally from the oppression of females that he located within marriage as a bourgeois institution, while allowing him to enjoy an unexamined asymmetry in power between himself and his domestic partners. It seems likely that both Mary and Lizzie Burns were lifelong illiterates.

In *The Origin of the Family,* Engels was equivocal on the subject of domestic duties, since he implied some residual division of labor by sex. He referred explicitly to a woman's "family duties," but exactly what these were, and what consequences they entailed for women and their public employment, are matters he did not raise. Nor did he discuss whether or not men have some domestic duties, and the consequences that this might entail. In personal correspondence throughout his life, he played the demanding male, jesting at his own domestic helplessness in order to secure the services of a female servant, unmarried female relative, or suitable divorcée to make fires and darn socks (Carver 1989, 148; see pp. 68-76).

Women in History

There is very little in Engels's *The Origin of the Family* that inspires much confidence today, though it must also be noted that it is difficult to say anything about prehistory today that is not a retracing of modern ideas and concerns. Preliterate societies leave artifacts behind, not ideas, and attempts to read culture—the realm of meaningful activities and narratives—off artifacts inevitably begin from assumptions necessarily of the "present" about how the "past" was constructed differently, and what practices and understandings within it are similar to those of the "present," all of which are necessarily derived from current experience and are perforce speculations (Shanks and Tilley 1987; see p. 3).

Engels's assumptions, which I have detailed above, lack persuasive justification and are obviously anachronistic. The single, worldwide chain of evolutionary development, combining notions of productive change with a version of natural selection, is methodologically suspect, precisely because it is merely assumed and not sufficiently examined against other approaches available at the time. The same is true of the natural division of labor between the sexes, the universality of matrilineal systems of kinship, and the connection between matrilineal kinship and social status. His assumptions about the differing sexual behavior of men and women are vague and ambiguous, since it is not clear whether they are supposed to be universal features of the two sexes based on physiological differences, or whether these generalizations admit counterexamples arising from aspects of social conditioning Engels did not investigate. While it is true that Engels declared the historicity and malleability of the sexual and kinship relations commonly categorized as "the family," this truth was hardly new or a secret, not least because Marx and Engels themselves had publicized it nearly forty years previously in the *Manifesto*.

The story of the overthrow of mother-right by father-right assigns to the individual males of a prehistoric communistic household a concept of inheritance that corresponds all too closely to the modern legal right that Engels takes to be a product of bourgeois society. His identification of monogamy with modern systems of private property, and other forms of marriage with the communistic household, is also unconvincing. What counts as communistic ownership was not detailed, and what counts as monogamy, apart from the enforcement of modern ideas of private property and inheritance, was not argued through.

More important, the very notions of what constitutes work within and outside a household, what makes an activity domestic or private as opposed to social or public, what makes resources and wealth external or internal to the household, how different sorts and amounts of work can be variously judged to be of different status, and how such judgments are to be evaluated, are matters that Engels did not satisfactorily explore. His generalizations reflected his own background and proclivities all too clearly and were untested against other experiences and viewpoints available in his own time. They have an authoritative and factual force only because that is the language in which he expressed himself, and it is easy for a reader to be carried along through a complex account.

Engels is more promising when he summarized the contemporary struggle for the emancipation of women, the necessity of establishing real social equality between the sexes. In his view, modern industry not only permits but requires the participation of women in production. However, when proletarian women have this opportunity, employment is presented in such a way that women who take part in public production and earn an independent wage cannot fulfill family duties, as he put it, and those fulfilling such duties in the private service of a family are excluded from public employment, independent earnings, and the advantages and higher social status that these bring. The same applies, so Engels said, in the professions, and the domination of men over women within the modern family will be brought into "full relief" only when both are equal before the law as it applies in the public sphere. The first premise for the emancipation of women is, Engels assumed, the "reintroduction of the entire female sex into public industry" and the reorganization of the economy so that productive resources, including labor, are not controlled and managed in families but are centrally calculated and directed, taking individual workers as the unit of society. The overall difficulty of reorganizing public industry along communist lines, as Engels saw them, was not discussed in this text (nor much discussed by Engels anyway). How the domestic sphere is to be made public was not even hinted at. Perhaps he envisaged communal catering and cleaning services, where work counts as public exactly as in the more obviously industrial activities (Engels 1980, 500–503).

Engels's analysis suffers from implicit biologism and explicit stereo-typing that are themselves indefensible. The biologism derives from his use of natural selection and deterministic assumptions about the behavior of women and men as important steps in his argument about the origins of women's oppression. Stereotyping appears in his account of what is sup-posed to be typical in the way that roles are assigned to women and men in productive and reproductive activities in society, however it is organized. Moreover, the relationship between what is typical and what is biologically determined was not addressed.

Engels accepted traditional ways of conceptualizing the public and the private, the economic and the noneconomic, and the political and the non-political that are not neutral with respect to the gender roles commonly assumed and enforced in his own society. In fact his work is innocent of one of the most interesting developments in feminist analysis, when these dichotomies are themselves declared problematic. Thus for Engels, a politi-cal and public sphere of economic relationships might still define and deval-ue a nonpolitical, private, and noneconomic sphere where some forms of oppression, against which feminists rightly protest, could very well contin-ue. Arguing that these distinctions and views were unavailable to him as he wrote does not save his text as usable theory, nor is it necessarily true in any case. Readings are conducted in the present, and one valid line of criticism must be the standards we choose to apply in our own time, leaving aside whether these ideas were available at all to any past individual, or whether that individual has perhaps some excuse for having missed them if they were there; or if they were not there, for not having invented them, as indeed someone finally did.

Conclusion

My contribution to the continuing debate about *The Origin of the Family* is to note that Engels did not make men problematic. Instead, he dissolved any problems that there might be with men into a developmental naturalism that effectively excused them all—as men. Thus, in prehistory, biology made men oppressors and women victims; but in historical times the class strug-gle made the bourgeoisie the oppressors and the proletariat the oppressed. Engels's transmutation of prehistorical naturalism into historical politics left men where they always were and validated a masculinity of convenience, much like the one he lived out (di Stefano 1991). More important, it left dominant masculinities and dominating males quite untouched. Content analysis may suggest that Engels's text is about women; narrative analysis suggests that he let men off the hook. *The Origin of the Family* constructs a feminism safe for men precisely because it presents, normalizes, and justifies a masculinist perspective.

More broadly, this chapter on Engels and the family illustrates how my reconceptualization of gender as the ways that sex and sexuality become political produces a different reading of a notable work of political theory, a different perspective on a famous political theorist, and (I hope) a different view of feminist politics. Engels's credentials as a pioneer feminist and a founder for Marxist feminism should now seem much more problematic. His focus on women is suspect in a number of ways.

First, the foregrounding of woman as object of study is not necessarily conducive to a perspective that accords them the same dignity in politics that male theorists characteristically accord to man, that is, men as a sex. The framing of such feminism as he has been credited with in terms of the family is an obvious clue to the way that reproduction is mapped onto woman, as if it were somehow only women who are involved. In his text, as in so many others, men seem to have a sexuality that backgrounds reproduction, and women a sexuality that enacts it. A perspective on gender that decouples reproduction (as biological sex) from sexuality (as behavior) reveals the lacunae that enable stereotypes to flourish. Insofar as feminists find themselves in agreement with Engels's text, they participate in this process.

Second, while Engels's perspective on men and women is conventionally gendered in terms of sexuality and reproduction, it actually erases the contemporary politics that occurs within those very gender boundaries. This happens because Engels subsumes female oppression in historical times into class oppression, by making women a class, and this simply dissolves intraclass difficulties between male and female proletarians into a politics of presumptive solidarity, rather than one that allows for polarization (see pp. 66–69). The apparatus of stereotypical male/female heterosexuality and Darwinian selection that precedes his political theory of the present is effectively unnecessary, and rather serves to frame his conclusions with the trappings of biological determinism and anthropological imperialism. Engels does nothing substantial in this text to address the questions that the contemporary women's movements put to the socialist parties of the time, however variously those movements were conceived.

Third, the division of the human story into a prehistory dominated by biology and selection and an economic history dominated by property and oppression enables Engels to construct a number of flattering images of female power and authority (one way that sex becomes political), yet put these images safely aside far from the present day, as there are no arguments within his overall framework of technological development for repeating prehistory. Moreover, such complexity as he introduces into this account—

a disjunction between work and respect—muddies the waters of the very proletarian politics that he was pursuing. Would he have argued that a social-ist value structure compensates disproportionate labor with genuine respect? I doubt it.

Fourth, Engels's focus on women enables him to keep men and their masculinities backgrounded and unproblematic. History overtakes biology when they move outside the family, where women are in control, and it is men who invent forms of production that create wealth and power. This inscribes not just a commonplace view of maleness but rather of a singular masculinity in which—at least in Engels's prehistory—all men naturally participated. Narratives of prehistory are notable for the way in which they deindividualize the human subject, reduce behavior to biology, and length-en time scales to such an extent that human consciousness becomes a func-tion of mysterious underlying forces, in ways that would never be assumed about humans in the present (Shanks and Tilly 1987). Alternatively, if we are going to theorize individuality, we must theorize gender (as the ways that sex and sexuality become power relations in society), and if we are going to theorize gender, then we must theorize masculinities. This means plurality, and not just the dominant sort, as otherwise the dynamics of gender power never get sufficiently and convincingly detailed. Had Engels theorized men more thoroughly and variously into the family, their exit from it would have looked less monolithic (mythical as all this is). The intraclass dynamics of proletarian politics would have looked more crucially violent (some men against women and other men) and more genuinely problematic (as it actu-ally was).

Having linked Engels the icon to the theory of the family, as I did in my remarks on how gender and class were intertwined in his own life, I have argued for a new view of the theorist. A supposed requirement to practice what you preach is merely trite, as no socialist or even reformer can live out, individually and in the present, what are supposed to be social goals for the future (Barrett 1983, 216). Rather, what can be gleaned from correspon-dence and memoirs concerning the theorist's family life—early years as a child and young adult, domestic affairs after leaving home, and continuing relationships with parents and siblings in later life—might reveal how theo-retical precepts are closely tracked as life is lived out, or alternatively how the recorded experience explicitly or implicitly contradicts a classic text. Engels's enthusiastic rendering of bourgeois values as a version of dominant masculinity was silent on a proletarian masculinity that presumably invert-ed the acquisitiveness that drives his account of economic development. Moreover, the way in which his own relationships—keeping proletarian women in the suburbs, rude comments about female servants—reproduced the very bourgeois values he condemned in print must necessarily color our reading of *The Origin of the Family* (see below, pp. 55–56, where the construction of political theory through biography is explored). The extent to which the traditional silence on these points is protected in standard commentaries or biographies—through selective quotation and failure to probe—is testimony to the tenacity with which icons are erected for worship in intellectual work and political life. The words on the page do not speak for themselves; we need idols to give them voice.

There are implications here for feminist politics. The first, I think, is that feminism should be even more iconoclastic. The second is that it should focus on the dynamics of gender oppression in a manner less simply polar with respect to two sexes understood as reproductive "opposites"; the extent to which these discussions are simply polar and implicitly reproductive merely reinscribes the view that female oppression is an effect of something in the male sex, rather than something that results from what some men do to women, and to each other. The latter perspective offers scope for alliance building within the family, as it is lived out in a multiplicity of relationships. The solution to oppression must lie in addressing gender as a power dynamic involving sex and sexuality, and not in searching for some supposed origin, which can only be symbolic, to gender trouble in biology or prehistory.

This is to say that new theories are required. Until we have credible and critical ways of theorizing masculinities, it will be as easy as ever to excuse men's oppressions within the family, private property, the state, and anywhere else, just as Engels managed to do. Moreover, new theories will have to challenge traditional conceptions of the public and the private, the political and the nonpolitical, the economic and noneconomic—as feminisms generally do in theory and in practice. As feminisms make men look different, so critical perspectives on masculinity/ies will make almost everything else look different.

In Chapter 3 I further this argument by looking at biography as an overarching genre through which political theory is constructed. This entails a conception of biography as lifeworld, which contrasts starkly with traditional constructions of the great thinker and his context. Developing an alternative framework for a biography—with reference to the way I have actually carried it out in the case of Engels—leads to a focus on the sense in which the historical contextualization in question is literally *his* context, given that, in the case of political theory, the authorial subjects involved are overwhelmingly male. Traditionally, maleness, masculinity/ies, and such personal matters are backgrounded or devalued in conventional commentary, and I reverse the movement of the present chapter (from classic text to author's life) by working in the next chapter in the opposite direction (from author's lifeworld to classic texts).

3

The Politics of the Personal in Political Biography

Political theory entails biography. This is because all the concepts employed in political theory have histories. In any given work, these histories may or may not be recounted. But even if intellectual history is denied, there are ways to fill it in. Indeed, it would be difficult for anyone to try to read in a contextless, historyless, cultureless way. Readers are not strictly confined by authorial terms of reference, and they bring what they already know, or wish to find out, to their reading of political theory.

Among the standard works of political theory are numerous contextualizing narratives about the great authors of the canon, and there are of course full-scale intellectual biographies and shorter studies. Hobbes and sovereignty, Mill and liberty, Marx and the class struggle—these names are among the most familiar. Theorizing society by rereading the classics has been strongly defended by Alexander (1987) on precisely the arguments that theory itself has a role in reinforcing and creating what we experience as social, that what is social is transmitted through texts as well as practice, and that particularly acute observers of society generate texts that are rightly and usefully reread, even if the kind of society they dealt with seems remote (see also Morgan 1992, 49–71). Where we have intellectual activity, we have authors; and where we have authors, we have biography—and autobiography.

I will address a number of issues not often confronted in political theory, and I will work this through by using material from my own biography of Friedrich Engels (1820–1895). I wish to make biography problematic in terms of what it is to give an account of a person's life and context. I also want to make biography more problematic as a genre than it is usually thought to be. Moreover, I aim to make the biographer just as problematic by arguing that form and content are authorially constructed, even when they appear to be dictated by external constraints. Most centrally, I comment on how a perspective, drawn from studies of gender and sexuality, can be applied to a male subject and his masculinity. This entails a discussion of Engels's own views on gender relations and gender politics, a portrait of relationships that were both personal and political, and an account of how these were intertwined with contemporary concepts of class.

Biographical Narrative

While not a statesman, Engels did participate in political action and was active in politics as a writer. He was part of the most influential intellectual partnership of all time, and he was phenomenally successful in his own right as a political pamphleteer. Additionally, some of his ideas were of a theoretical character and survived him in classic works. Indeed, posthumous readings of them have eclipsed his actual activities in politics as a speech maker and organizer, as well as his contemporary influence on others through conversation, correspondence, journalism, and books. In effect he had, and still has, a function in twentieth-century politics and beyond, insofar as in contemporary eyes he is a figure of authority, or alternatively a scapegoat.

Biography is, of course, historical narrative, and in recent years the author-narrative-subject-reader-audience nexus has been questioned or deconstructed (White 1987). Subjects, such as biographical ones, are said to be ultimately inaccessible, in that their inner motives could never have been projected into some external evidence, accessible to a biographer, without remainder or distortion. Meaning is said to lie solely in narrative as read by different interpreters, not in any matching between concept and object. Different meanings are said to arise in different readers, as they put their own constructions on narratives. The author is therefore said to be dead (Murphy 1989).

Or rather, there is now enormous suspicion of authors. They are no longer regarded even in principle as reliable media through which facts about subjects can reach an audience. Authors' assumptions and judgments are scrutinized, presumed to be the subtext or hidden agenda of narratives; texts are said to incorporate absences as well as presences (Skinner 1988, 272–273). Scholarly biographies, heavy with footnotes and learning, are no exception.

Narrative is crucial to understanding; neither texts nor lives are strings of propositions. Texts are related to arguments and lives to motives, as Skinner and others have argued. Both lives and texts must be considered much more carefully now, as the age of philosophical innocence for political biographers is over. In a review of Martin Gilbert's *Churchill: A Life,* Ben Pimlott (biographer of Hugh Dalton and Harold Wilson) comments on the formal construction of biography, arguing that it must be more than a chronological mirroring of what survives among papers and recollections:

> Yet lives have more than a temporal dimension to them. They contain
> themes, patterns and conflicts which cannot be considered merely as a
> series of disparate events. Thus, in a book which seeks to provide "a full
> and rounded picture" we deserve a chapter—even though it would break
> the chronology—on Churchill's unusually happy marriage and family life
> [Pimlott 1991].

In my narrative, an intellectual and political biography of Engels
(Carver 1989), I confront the reader with myself as biographer by intruding
into the text-as-mirror and listing questions I propose to answer. I give guid-
ing questions for the work as a whole, so that the reader will know why I
undertook it; and I give more-specific questions for each chapter, or sometimes pair of chapters. I recognize that readers should not be burdened with
unwanted autobiography, but it is fair to identify oneself to an audience as
having some things in mind quite specifically, and not others. The reader
should be aware that the biography emerges from a biographer with inten-
tions, and not from some godlike consciousness, omniscient and
omnipresent.

I think it likely that readers find it restful to assume that biographers are
all-knowing because they have burrowed into every archive, and all-wise
because they have selected just what is necessary to make the narrative go.
Biographers and readers both find it easy to pretend that the biographer is a
"time lord," opening a "time tunnel" down which readers can peer in utter
transparency and thus recapture the past as it was. In a sense there is a conspiracy of trust between biographer and audience. This, in my view, should
be replaced by mutual suspicion, as otherwise a mutual tendency to intellectual laziness takes over.

The Narrative Frame

Biographies are traditionally but only seemingly framed by the birth and
death of the subject. Generally, the life as presented in a biographical narrative is preceded by brief lives of forebears and identification of influences,
whether persons or ideas or books. This may extend to essays on the spirit
of the times or cultural tradition or whatever strikes the writer as relevant,
useful, and properly validated. All these devices serve to determine the biographical subject's consciousness and to discount that subject's own will. To
counter this common way of conceptualizing the subject, I deliberately
allude to the careers of others in the Engels family who were the "products"
of virtually identical "influences," but were never remotely like Friedrich in
terms of what they attempted, accomplished, or even thought, so far as is
known (Carver 1989, 1–5).

Indeed, what is known becomes a major theme in my work, in that I also remind the reader that history, including biography, is an archeological exercise. Only certain kinds of materials, and only certain exemplars at that, happen to have survived to the present. Thus, one has to be extremely careful in drawing definitive conclusions about the subject on the basis of whatever materials happen to have been preserved. Curiously, the business of looking for new materials, and for making use of chance discoveries, often counts in narratives about biographers as an opportunity to revise or overturn the deterministically structured accounts already produced—with a new and even contradictory one couched in much the same terms. The tentative character of biographical representations of lives, and the fluid and continuing character of biographizing as a practice, ought surely to be acknowledged with some force, not merely noticed and disregarded.

Thus, I draw the conclusion, concerning some matters in the Engels biography, that surviving materials allow us merely to note an ambiguity or unsolved problem; and, concerning other issues, I deliberately draw a variety of contrasting conclusions, since it seems to me that several plausible narratives are compatible with the evidence. I also speculate on the nature and content of materials, and indeed of immaterial things like conversations that did not, or could not, have survived as they happened at the time. Obviously, the reader has to be warned that these are speculations, but it is extremely important in my approach that such absences should be flagged for attention. By working from what is known to what is unknown, however, some speculations can be promoted as more plausible than others. I mention this particularly because such black-hole categories as unrecorded conversations have been used in Marx-Engels studies to fill out hypotheses in ways that conform more closely to the biographer's views than to the materials that have survived (Shanks and Tilley 1987; Carver 1983, 118–151).

The death of the subject comes traditionally at the close of the biography, though not at the absolute end, as the biographical frame generally includes the subject's posthumous influence. During their own lifetimes, biographical subjects are events in other people's lives, and they continue in that role after their deaths. They sometimes continue to publish their works, and they become objects of interpretation. In some senses, then, it does not matter much whether the great thinker is dead or alive.

Engels is particularly interesting in this respect, as he established an interpretative context around himself ("Marx's junior partner") and around Marx (the "materialist philosopher who inverted Hegel," the "Darwin of the social sciences," the "revolutionary fighter" for communism). Moreover, inasmuch as Engels's biographers determined his consciousness through traditional narrative methods, so in turn did he attempt to determine—quite successfully for many years—the consciousness of his biographers. He did this by establishing a narrative about himself in relation to Marx; about

Marx in relation to politics; and about his own, his and Marx's, and Marx's own works in relation to philosophy and science (Carver 1983).

Narrative Time

Narrative time in biography often moves in ways of which the biographer is perhaps not conscious, or at least not too willing to inform the reader. Narrative time is really space on the printed page, as biographers dwell longer (in terms of words to be read) on some topics than on others. An attempt by a biographer to give narrative weight to certain aspects of a life rather than others may well be subverted by crude and often intuitive judgments made by readers based on pages of printed space or time needed to read it. A number of different considerations may be dictating the structure of the recovered life in this sense.

One consideration is simply the amount of material to which the biographer has access; for example, there may be enormous amounts of late correspondence after a subject has become famous, but little juvenilia for the inverse reason. Another is how the biographer periodizes the recovered life. This, of course, reflects the overall view that the biographer takes of the subject's career, and that naturally reflects what the biographer thinks is important about the subject. What was actually important to the subject at any given time in attempting to determine his or her life tends to fade out here, and the importance of the subject, or the subject's writings, or the idea of the subject, as these appear in the later lives of others, tends to take center stage in the narrative. Indeed, it is usually within the lives of others around the biographical subject that biographical traditions begin to emerge. As I argue in Chapter 4, these are notoriously difficult to dislodge, and they are best construed as indelible texts that must be acknowledged and confronted rather than merely reproduced.

The importance of the subject in history (as lived out by other people) thus becomes the subject's narrative life within the biographical frame, and I strove not to allow that to pass unacknowledged in my work. Partly this is because Engels's reputation and influence are well documented elsewhere; partly this is because I did not want events or activities as they occurred in his life to assume an anachronistic importance; and partly I wished to experiment with a biography that was rooted in life as lived by the subject in order to create a contrast with traditional narrative, which I regard as frankly mythological, hagiographical, and self-referential.

Why the biographer thinks some things are important about the subject, and not others, is often not explicitly revealed but absorbed within the conspiracy of trust between author and reader to which I referred earlier (p. 57). Some biographers may regard what is important about the subject as already fixed, and new biographies merely add to facts already known an interpretation that may (sometimes feebly) be described as fresh. But the subject remains a great politician or poet or writer or whatever, just as we originally thought. In that way biographers reproduce interpretative traditions, and those traditions dictate what among the subject's remains is public and supposedly lasting, and what is private and presumably trivial.

An interpretative tradition thus acts to determine the subject's consciousness retrospectively, and to dull any skepticism in the reader. For example, Engels could never have wanted to be an artist or make a career in the theater (though we have his early sketchbooks and a libretto—*Rienzi*—written at about the same time as Wagner's). Indeed, we do not know what his career plans were in his early youth; perhaps he did not know either. Biographers generally race through juvenilia at blinding speed, unless it happens to foreshadow later activities that posterity has judged important. Better biographers make gestures denying teleology, but I am not persuaded that they succeed, or succeed with sufficient obviousness, in showing the reader that life-as-lived-at-the-time did not have, nor could it have had, the meanings that interpretative traditions subsequently supply.

Posterity plays a large role in dictating narrative space, in that books or manuscripts that were of little importance to anyone, perhaps even the subject at the time, sometimes become important events in the narrative world; consider *The German Ideology* manuscripts in Engels's hand that went unpublished (and unwanted) for many years. The biographer's audience may be told that the subject's ignorant contemporaries had no idea what they were missing. The overwhelming impression that readers take away from such narratives is that the subject is yet another lonely genius adrift in an ungrateful world. This, of course, devalues the subject's contemporaries and abstracts the subject out of any plausible conception of the everyday activities and circumstances in which a life actually consists. The subject's own quite understandable uncertainties do not get communicated. Consciousness can hardly be as unitary and questing as biographers allow us to believe, as it is in their interests to assimilate their biographical subject to the rank of genius. Biography itself erases that obscurity into which the lives of ordinary people are generally assumed to descend.

Characters and Dramaturgy

In writing an intellectual biography of Engels, I decided to confront the reader directly, and initially, with my subject's continuing, everyday relationships, as all his life he was a son or brother, an uncle, lover, or friend to a large number of people, relatively few of whom were communists (who were in any case extremely disparate characters). Bringing these associates back to life is obviously particularly difficult, as they exist for us only in letters and memoirs. The letters extant are almost wholly those written by Engels, rather than by his correspondents, and the memoirs of him that are available were almost wholly composed within the interpretative tradition that he himself helped to create. While he is perhaps somewhat unusual in this respect, it also seems likely that there is more of this self-biographizing from beyond the grave than is generally acknowledged.

Yet there is a cast of supposedly unimportant characters in Engels's life, as in everyone's. Few biographers are interested in housekeepers, unmarried sisters, elderly mothers, wholly domestic spouses or partners, and so forth. I decided to bring them in ahead of the more famous names that form a central part of the narrative tradition, as it was with the nonfamous that the subject's everyday life was lived, and of course the subject in this case was nonfamous himself till very late in life. Further, these persons clearly occupied an enormous amount of his time. This is not to say that I could find much of them to recover, but I thought they should be resurrected from silence and exhibited to the reader in order to dramatize the distinction between the subject's lived experience and the narrative life constructed by a biographer. In the case of a male subject for a biographer, most of these relatively silent characters are bound to be women (see pp. 65–77).

Drama plays a very large role in interpretative traditions, in that some events are emphasized—independently of the space they occupy in the book—by the biographer, so that the reader can be apprised of turning points, or setbacks, or other cruces in the life. The initial Marx-Engels meetings are a case in point, as Engels's early life is generally conceptualized such that his first meeting with Marx was poignantly cold. His second meeting, by dramatic contrast, is presented as the denouement of his previous activities and the overture to his real life as posterity sees it (Carver 1989, 95–101). Indeed, the fact that these events are portrayed as Marx-Engels meetings, even in biographies of the latter, gives the game away, in that the focus of most work on Engels, even biographical work, is really Marx, not the subject himself!

I worked hard to make the meetings Engels-Marx meetings; to make Marx one character in Engels's life; and to keep Marx from taking over the narrative, as he often threatened to do. Interpretative traditions are the very stuff of what one takes for granted, and eternal vigilance is extremely difficult to achieve. At the same time, modern readers naturally relate Engels to Marx, and I took care in considering their early years to construct detailed comparisons between Marx's early achievements (actually rather modest) and Engels's interests and output (far more impressive) (Carver 1989, 175).

These dramatic moments are, of course, constructs, often traceable to memoirists and early biographers. Plausibly, the people involved in these circumstances had little sense at the time of this importance, which was constructed much later. Their actions and reactions within the narrative drama thus move them into a world-historical realm, where most readers would like them to be, and where they never actually were. Otherwise they would seem not merely unimportant but rather ambiguous and indeterminate. This again has the effect of determining the consciousness of individuals, who were once real, and recovering them to readers today as characters in a prose drama. Transfer to the stage and screen is thus but a step away, though it is difficult to think of a bio-pic that is other than anachronistic and teleological in worse ways than most written biographies.

Narrative Purpose

What a biography is actually for should always be an issue for biographer and reader, and at least in the biography of Engels I tried to make it so. Worship or denigration of the subject seems to me to be an insufficient motive for writing a biography, especially when the order of service or alternatively auto da fé is so relentlessly laid down by predecessors. Modern theories of structuration take socialization and agency with equal seriousness, and I was interested to show the reader the extent to which a supposedly familiar character could be reconstructed as a choice-making agent (Giddens 1979; Callinicos 1987). In my narrative, Engels is someone who experimented with ideas and relationships, a person who lived out ambiguities of which he was aware, a politician who retreated from action to writing. Ironically, Engels was himself the author of a deterministic philosophy, and an advocate of highly wilful agency, and thus set the terms, to some extent, for contemporary attempts to resolve this issue theoretically.

Engels's early works reveal the indeterminacy of the subject's mind and show the supposed formative process as contingent on circumstances quite outside himself or herself and just as indeterminate. While human activity is unlikely to be random, in the true sense, there is certainly an element of unpredictability that must be presumed, as we each presume it about ourselves and our own decisions. No one lives life as if determinism were true, and similarly we cannot successfully present ourselves as completely unconstrained by the ideas of others, even as interpreted in our own consciousness.

Engels's father, for instance, made deliberate decisions to constrain his son. These were just the sort of decisions that one would have expected an industrialist of the Ruhr to have made at that time. In turn, Engels junior, while constrained physically, financially, and emotionally within institutions and assumptions set by others, chose to broaden his experience in quite contrary ways. My narrative brings out the indeterminacy and ambiguity of these situations and choices in ways that make his early years more lively and his later ones more controversial. But I took him to be somewhat less of an agent after he was twenty-four, in that he was demonstrably less experimental, and in particular he kept himself in circumstances that he did not alter in fundamental ways, personally, politically, and intellectually.

One of the other themes I chose to explore in my biography concerns the extent to which writing and politics are coincident activities, and the extent to which one may preclude the other. Literary biographers perhaps have a similar problem when confronting works of literature that, for the subject, were also ways of making a living in the basest sense. Even where the issue is raised, the gravity and necessity of the subject's struggles with quotidian economics often pale before the presumed world-historical context of lasting achievement in which the biographer's narrative is located. The narrative tradition about Engels decrees that his written words were political acts, and that important political acts were quite naturally acts of publication, specifically the publication of works that have lasted and are standard on the library shelves. In the case of Engels some of those published works could do with a decent burial, or so I argue in Chapter 2 above, and others should be dusted off, as the current situation—in which I somewhat authoritatively locate myself and my readers—now differs in social and political terms from the context in which the largely unchanging interpretative tradition was established. These considerations support my allocation of one-half of the narrative space-time to hitherto little-regarded early works.

My investigation of the situation surrounding Engels's early works exposed the extent to which the subject engaged in political activities that were not themselves the business of writing and publishing major works. This produced in my narrative as a whole something like the hallowed formative pattern of development—but in reverse. That is, the subject successively withdrew from various activities and became in a sense less successful as chronological time went on. As Engels's career proceeded he lost skills and interests, such as speech making to the public and party-political organizing among workers. In his early days of practical political activity he had upbraided his principal collaborator, Marx, for undue bookishness, inopportune reluctance to engage with real workers, and neglect of day-to-day politics. Later he dropped this line of criticism, as it would have applied all too closely to himself, and indeed he dropped all lines of criticism of Marx, as he had hitched his own career to Marx's in no uncertain terms (Carver 1989, 172–260).

This allocation of narrative space did not go without criticism. David McLellan (1990) in particular noted my "full and insightful treatment of the genesis of Engels's thought and of his politics" but commented that it was "bought at the price of a severe neglect of many of Engels's later (and more influential) works." "Carver," he says, "almost seems deliberately *not* to be interested in those of Engels's works that have attracted most subsequent attention," but he concedes that this was intended as a tactic for redressing a perceived imbalance in the way that Engels had heretofore been treated. Yet following the track of a comprehensive biography endorsed by McLellan would have reproduced a number of confusions.

For a start, there is a distinction between life and legacy, and writing the posthumous reception and evaluation of various lifeworks back into the biographical frame actually overwrites the subject's lived experience with those of a later, ghostly figure—the world-historical Engels created by the very enthusiasm and interest his works provoked in others in the decades following his death. The same is true of his political contacts, in that the precarious and unformed character of these associations, mostly in correspondence, become events in a founding narrative concerning structures of influence that existed only after Engels's own existence had ceased. The biography of Marxist socialism as a movement seems to me to be one thing, and a biography of Engels the man quite another.

Moreover, my argument was that Engels's late works were largely realizations of material from his earlier days, which had previously been analyzed within the earlier chapters of the biography. This would have been undone by allocating textual space to the late works in proportion to their physical dimensions as books or to their supposed importance and influence after their author's demise. And in terms of my view of the trajectory of Engels's activities and development, it would have been disastrous to treat them as masterpieces, since they simply lack the freshness and intensity characteristic of the earlier works from which they derived.

Of course, this is the imposition of a biographer's view of the subject's character upon the recovered life as a whole, but at least it is out in the open. Merely allocating narrative space in accordance with a canon of great books, and then justifying this in circular terms by arguing that tradition requires this arrangement, pushes all the problems of judgment into a realm of unchangeable narrative and immovable genre.

Narrative and Experience

My organization of narrative time introduces a further element of lived experience into biography, in that perceived time, when we face new circumstances, slows down, and, conversely, routinized events seem to flow swiftly. This perspective is delineated in *The Magic Mountain,* as Hans Castorp's arrival and early encounters at the sanatorium are supposedly experienced more slowly by the character himself than events taking place later, when the situation is more familiar (Mann 1988, 541–545). The narrative space presented in tactile form to the reader reflects this lived experience rather than strictly equal units of chronology. I judged the later years of my subject to be somewhat routine, and so cut down the narrative space they occupied. This telescopes chronological time and treats the sheer amount of material that remains from that period in a highly selective manner. The reader is warned of this and is referred to the literature that exists outside the biography. Moreover, I aimed to make the biography an introduction to and perspective on Engels's works, rather than a substitute for reading them to which the intellectually lazy might resort.

My narrative is also methodologically discontinuous, and critics will probably take this to be further evidence of an unwanted authorial intrusion into the traditional way that narrative and time interact in biography. I treated my subject's early years (till he was twenty-four) in a narrative that combined thematic and chronological exposition. For his life in maturity, I adopted a technique of inverse nesting. Most biographies of figures similar to mine prioritize their intellectual life and introduce their politics and personal quirks as the narrative proceeds, in order to provide useful motives for the subject and light relief for the reader. By contrast, I chose to survey the mature years of the subject's personal life, from age twenty-four through his seventy-fifth year, in a central chapter. (I confess I could not kill him off by mentioning the word *death* midway through the book.) Successive chapters on his political activities, including a convenient clutch of minor writings, and on his intellectual major writings, bring the narrative to the point of conclusion. In that way, the personal and political performative contexts of his thought are set out in advance (Skinner 1988).

Yet for me, Engels's enduring legacy, if such it proves, no longer necessarily lies in those works, but elsewhere, particularly in his early revolutionary constitutionalism, his forays into party politics, and his concern with the causes and consequences of economic stratification in industrial societies (Carver 1992). I hope that some readers might be at least a little grateful for sparing them extended discussions of *Anti-Dühring* and *Dialectics of Nature*. Those works were historically important in the decades following Engels's death, and this is not to be denied. However, I take it that what is important for us about Engels can itself be reinterpreted, because who we are, and what "important" means, can be expected to change over time, perhaps profoundly.

Masculinity, Gender Politics, and Sexuality

Modern narratives of self and identity presume that we have public and private selves, that the latter are domestically located for the most part, and that within the innermost depths of the private self there are drives and yearnings for fulfillment of a sexual character (Evans 1993). This is a sociological generalization and could well be untrue of any individual. Its applicability to anyone who lived before Freud is questionable. For those reasons, I am precisely suggesting that the search through what remains of Engels's life for such an inner self would be anachronistic and foolish. Nonetheless, such biographical comments as there are on such personal issues seem to be very much of this character, or to be simply salacious and titillating. Rather, I tried to use a modern perspective on gender politics and sexuality to reread the record and indeed to rethink what the record actually is. Thus, within the central section on Engels's personal life—which was in fact the realm where most of his time was necessarily spent—I developed the following discussion, which I offer as illustrative of what a gendered perspective on men can accomplish. As Hearn and Collinson (1994, 112) note,

> political analysis and personal experience are confronting issues very similar to those of theoretical analysis. We find that the complexities of our own personal and biographical stories mirror these political and theoretical complexities. The interrogation of biography and autobiography is an important and necessary aspect of the interrogation of social divisions, in this case with respect to men and masculinities.

As one might expect, the extant record from Engels on personal matters, and from other sources about Engels that would give us outsiders' accounts, do not begin until a certain stage in his life, and then at that point in a specific context that is in no way a beginning. I am not attempting a psychobiography based on these materials as a way of filling in the gaps and constructing a personality for Engels around such evidence as survives and such speculation as can be justified. Rather, I am offering a reading of such written materials as I think bear on these issues. As can be seen from the starting point of my narrative, this is in no way a biographer's portrait, rounded as the genre allows. But it does contain my own interpretation of what Engels was like as a man (public man and private man) with respect to gender relations on the male/female, heterosexual/homosexual model, with respect to the gender politics of female emancipation current at the time, with respect to relationships with women and men within a context of dominant, heterosexual masculinity, and with particular respect to how those structures of opinion and modes of behavior interacted with the circumstances of social class he encountered in everyday life.

Engels: Sexual Politics and Sexual Practice

Engels's earliest remarks about women, so far as they are preserved, were made in the context of the struggle for female emancipation as it existed in the 1830s, when he was a teenager. As perceived by the young Engels, this was part of the struggle for democratic rights in politics and public life. Among prominent radicals—almost wholly male, of course—rights for women were associated with sexual liberation. They argued that women should have proper recognition as human subjects and equal intellects who could exercise choice over their lives with respect to sexual affairs, marriage, and divorce. Engels supported these causes, admittedly with what seems today a large amount of residual male chauvinism. One of his letters of 1839, when he was almost nineteen and a supporter of the Young Germany movement, caricatured the "Emancipation of Women" as a cigar-smoking female exposing her backside, and the "Emancipation of the Flesh" as a male bearing a priapic flagpole from which female undergarments (?) are displayed (Marx and Engels 1976–, 2:453).

As a youthful communist, Engels identified the revolutionary reform of heterosexual relations with the liberty of the individual, reporting this to English readers in 1843, when he was twenty-three. His early articles in German on political economy and the factory system, beginning when he was eighteen, reveal considerable sensitivity to the plight of children—obviously weak and dependent—and women, who seemed to some extent to fall into that category as well. In these early writings, communists and working people were generally chaps, lads, and men. His sensitivity to the woman question and to the particular horrors of factory work for females must be set against his presumption that political actors are male and that women are the weaker sex, as otherwise his context is seriously misconstrued.

Of course, in Engels's time political actors were in fact overwhelmingly male, so his references to political actors as generally male are not surprising. Indeed, it would have been surprising for him to refer to women as political actors on terms of equality with men, or even to think of advocating this in full, as the notion of equal participation in public life for women had hardly surfaced. The ideas were there, but public representation of them was not. It was easy for Engels—as for virtually everyone else—not to see the issue of democratic participation in politics as one of complete equality between the sexes, anyway, because of the prevailing assumption that female nature was essentially domestic. Housework, child rearing, caring for family members, and so forth were taken to be women's proper functions in society (Walby 1990).

The prevailing view of woman's lowly role—and the counterbalancing dignity of woman's work—was by no means inconsistent with liberal views stressing the liberty of the individual, because male and female individuals were taken to have different natures and therefore different spheres in which liberty was relevant. Engels's "Description of Recently Founded Communist Colonies still in Existence," written in German in October 1844 (when he was twenty-four), contained an approving account of Owenite communal living arrangements that expressed this outlook succinctly:

> The members [?] live together in a large house, each with a separate [?]
> bedroom, which is most comfortably furnished; the housekeeping is done
> for all of them together by some of the women [!], and this, of course, saves
> a great deal of expense, time and trouble [Marx and Engels 1976–, 4:226].

The most likely reading in context of this ambiguous passage is that Engels
was conceptualizing the members of the community as males, each fur-
nished with a bedroom and a woman, the women then undertaking the
domestic labor of the commune collectively. Similar presumptions reappear
in *The Origin of the Family, Private Property and the State,* published by
Engels some forty years later in 1884, when he took up the historical position of women in detail and incidentally made slightingly homophobic references to boy-love and pederasty, a rare reference to a sexuality that might
be in any way "other" (see pp. 46–48, 78 92).

In *The Origin of the Family,* Engels argued that the first premise for the
emancipation of women in modern society is their reintroduction into public industry. In his view, the reorganization of the domestic sphere as an
industrial activity, including communal catering and cleaning services,
would have to follow. Even so, he referred explicitly to women's family
duties but did not give a detailed account—childbearing and the care of
small children are obvious guesses—nor did he consider how the performance of these duties might then undercut equal participation for women in
community life. The issue of men's domestic duties did not arise at all, possibly because he really thought that there were none to discuss, or possibly
because his own circumstances made this kind of oversight an easy one for
him (see pp. 69–76).

Engels lived in a world—by no means vanished—where lowly domestic tasks are generally done by housewives, female relations, maidservants,
and housekeepers who tidy up. In 1852 (when he was thirty-two), for
instance, he wrote from Manchester to his married sister, Marie Blank, in
London inquiring about their little sister Elise, then about eighteen and
unmarried, connecting these four categories of female, one way or another,
with his domestic needs.

> What is Elise up to? If she's a good cook, and can darn stockings, she
> might well come over here [to Manchester] after Christmas and keep house
> for me. . . . Elise would undoubtedly be able to do the honours of the house
> quite famously, while all your old stick-in-the-mud bachelor has is an
> ancient, crotchety, six-foot-tall, skin-and-bone, intimidating, snarling,
> blear-eyed, doddery, unkempt, ex-kitchen maid of a housekeeper, but never
> a wife, despite his gallantries at concerts, balls and suchlike [Marx and
> Engels 1976–, 39:249].

Even if there is an element of dated (and tasteless) jest in some of these remarks, they nonetheless illustrate Engels's consistent assumption that women are essentially domestic creatures, and that men are the natural recipients of their services, waged or otherwise. Moreover, he was markedly more respectful throughout his life in his remarks concerning wives and female relations than in his comments on maidservants and housekeepers. His sister's (physical?) description of her new maids made him "eager to see them," and the housekeeper (unnamed) in Manchester was referred to as a "witch." He did not see women as a comprehensive group in any real sense, but instead saw broad categories of females, who were then the subject of commonplace discourse: solicitous concern for female relations; lustful appreciation for serving maids; abusive dislike for housekeepers (Marx and Engels 1976–, 38:270, 515).

Engels: Class and Heterosexuality

There were more-intimate relationships with women in Engels's life. In 1844, after returning from Manchester to the family home in Barmen, the twenty-four-year-old Engels reported to his new friend, Marx, that he had been involved in an unhappy love affair. However, nothing further is known about this girlfriend or just possibly fiancée. But in his 1852 letter to his sister, the phrase "never a wife" throws into relief another major ambiguity in his personal life. This is because to his brother-in-law, Emil Blank, and others in communist circles he had already announced a "wife"—Mary Burns (c. 1823–1863) (Marx and Engels 1976–, 38:37).

Mary was an Irish-born mill worker whom Engels met in Manchester, so it is assumed, when he was working there between 1842 and 1844 (aged twenty-two to twenty-four). This is the time when, according to his own account, he was making personal visits to the homes of the proletariat, and Mary was possibly his guide. For Engels, she did not occupy one of the categories of female enumerated above. She was a mill girl who worked outside the home in modern industry, and so she was not a female relation, maid, or housekeeper. Neither was she a wife (or girlfriend or fiancée) as understood at home, because she and Engels were never legally married or even continuously coresident. Instead she was an "honorary Mrs.," his sexual partner—so we presume—and political associate, who accompanied him to Brussels in 1845 at the start of his communist career. During his subsequent time in Paris and Cologne—a period that is very well documented—she almost disappears from view.

In the 1850s and early 1860s Mary was maintained by Engels in a domestic establishment in Ardwick in suburban Manchester separate from his lodgings near the center. Crudely this made her his mistress, "kept" in semisecrecy away from his public life with his employers, Ermen and

Engels (the family firm), the Albert Club, the Manchester Athenaeum, the Cheshire Hunt, the Schiller Anstalt, and other middle-class obligations and amusements. An unsuitable marriage with a working-class and very possibly illiterate Irish girl would have threatened Engels's position in these institutions, as he could have been drummed out of the purely social ones and penalized financially on the business side. When his circumstances were discovered by his "philistine" (his judgment) associates, he was not pleased. Had the two been married, the working-class Mary would of course have had no position in polite society, and her removal to middle-class circumstances would probably have deprived her of friends and family in the Irish community (Marx and Engels 1976–, 39:443).

Engels's family reacted with almost speechless horror to these possibilities early on. In December 1848, during an enforced absence from Germany as a result of his revolutionary and communistic activities, some of his belongings arrived at home from Cologne while his father was away. That was just as well, his mother wrote, because she had discovered various letters that she proposed to withhold from Friedrich senior.

> I consider it unnecessary to tell him everything I know, but if asked I do not knowingly tell anything but the *truth*. . . . Amongst the letters in your trunk I found one addressed to "Madame Engels" and one from a lady to yourself, written in French, though from Cologne [probably from Félicité André—see pp. 71–72]. . . . Both these letters I burnt unread. . . . Do not write to me about it, for I am most anxious that your father should hear nothing. . . . Later on, perhaps, you might give me an explanation by word of mouth. But I only wish to hear the truth.

Characteristically she continued, "If you cannot tell me that, it would be better for us not to speak at all on the subject." A bride from an unsuitable background would not have been a welcome addition to the family circle in purely social terms, and in financial terms—the management of current property and the transmission of inheritance—the idea was unthinkable (Marx and Engels 1976–, 38:545).

Some of Engels's communist associates were not at all amused that a mill owner's son was taking advantage, so it seemed, of a factory girl who had nothing to sell but her labor in that most personal of ways. The émigré Stephan Born (pseud. Simon Buttermilch, 1824–1898), a German typesetter and one of the Brussels communists, recounted that Marx and his wife had attended a workers' association meeting in late 1847 or early 1848 at which Engels had arrived with a lady, unnamed but presumed to be Mary Burns. She had joined Engels *à deux* (Mrs. Jenny Marx's reference to the matter) in Brussels sometime in the latter part of 1845, after Engels's trip during the summer to Manchester in company with Marx. In memoirs written long after the event, Born recalled that Marx had indicated by glances and smiles that his wife would not meet Engels's companion.

Obviously there is some room for doubt here concerning exactly what was going on. Born drew the conclusion that Marx's "noble lady" (the von Westphalens had aristocratic connections) held strict views about marriage and morals. But there is room for doubt here as well, because Born may have misunderstood her intention—if such it was—of not acknowledging Engels's "wife" in public, even among communists. Born continued his recollections by commenting that Engels should not have brought his mistress to the gathering at all, as it was a tactless reminder to workers that the sons of rich mill owners were often accused of using working-class women and girls for their own pleasure (Marx and Engels 1976–, 38:529; Henderson 1976, 1:104).

Yet the Marx family and the Engels ménage maintained adjoining accommodation in various locations and for a time stayed in the same inn in Brussels, where Engels's friend Georg Weerth (1822–1856)—another communist businessman working at times in England—gave the impression that there was nothing untoward in the close association. In a letter to his mother in 1846 he observed:

> The famous Marx is living in the room opposite to mine with his very beautiful and well-educated wife and two bonny children. Fried[rich] Engels, whose book on England you have read, is staying here too. His wife is an English [*sic*] girl from Manchester so we converse half in English and half in German (Gemkow 1972, 116–117).

In the later 1840s Engels was not shy in declaring in correspondence that he was occupying himself with girls, as Mary did not accompany him on his trips to Paris on behalf of the Brussels communists. In particular, he once boasted of two conquests to Marx. This happened when, as Engels had it, Sibylle Hess—the wife of his former mentor Moses Hess—conceived a passion for him that he did not return. Meanwhile Hess went into a jealous rage—not at all the first—over his wife's infatuation and reportedly accused Engels of rape. Engels portrayed this accusation as absurd, since he had been the one pursued, and in any case Hess, said Engels, was "perfectly at liberty . . . to avenge himself on all my present, past and future mistresses," and then listed two:

> 1) the Flemish giantess who lives at my former lodgings . . . whose name is Mademoiselle Joséphine, and 2) a Frenchwoman, Mademoiselle Félicie [Félicité André] who, on Sunday, the 23rd of this month, will be arriving in Brussels by the first train from Cologne on her way to Paris. It would be bad luck if he were to succeed with neither. . . . I will give him fair play.

During the early days of the 1848 revolution in Paris, Engels and Félicité André were living at the same address (Marx and Engels 1976–, 38:153, 166).

Certainly, Marx seemed to take Engels's relationship with Mary Burns to be rather casual, even in the 1850s. Engels had written on 29 January 1851 that Marx's previous letter had been mislaid by his "old witch of a landlady" in a pile of books. "Had I been studying Russian this month instead of physiology," Engels continued, "this wouldn't have happened." Marx inquired lubriciously on 3 February, "Is it on Mary you're studying physiology, or elsewhere?" Engels's reply of 5 February offered no reproof, but on 13 February Engels described himself to Marx in English as a "bachelor" and said that he was bored. During the cotton crisis of the early 1860s, caused by the U.S. Civil War, Engels reported to Marx that, as the firm had no orders, he was working only half the time and living almost all the time with Mary "so as to spend as little money as possible." "Unfortunately," he continued, "I can't dispense with my lodgings, otherwise I should move in with her altogether." Accommodation for Mary and her sister Lizzie or Lizzy (otherwise Lydia, 1827–1878) was rented in the name of "Frederick Boardman," and Mary was "Mrs. Boardman." Lizzie kept house for the "married couple," acting the unmarried female relation in a household that was neither respectably middle class nor conventionally proletarian—nor egalitarian by modern standards. By Engels's standards, it may have represented some contemporary approach to communism, as it was a cross-class alliance between workers in industry, albeit very much on his own terms in the domestic arrangements (Marx and Engels 1976–, 38:270–281, 290, 41:344, 370, 634 n. 425).

Engels: Friendship and Retrospection

When Mary died suddenly of heart disease—at about forty-one—she was almost overlooked by the Marxes, and for that Engels rebuked his friend Karl quite sharply. But as the Marxes were not generally insensitive, that rebuke may tell us something about the way Engels's relationship appeared to outsiders. Evidently he had failed to make his regard for Mary completely clear to those who in all other matters were his intimates. On 7 January 1863 Engels wrote very briefly: "Mary is dead. . . . I simply can't convey what I feel. The poor girl loved me with all her heart." Marx responded by return on the eighth, "The news of Mary's death surprised no less than it dismayed me. She was so good-natured, witty and closely attached to you." He then launched into yet another heartrending account of his family's financial embarrassments and his attempts to raise money, saying, "Instead of Mary, ought it not to have been my mother?" He was obviously expecting a legacy.

Five days after Marx's urgent pleas, Engels replied, on the thirteenth, referring to Marx's "frosty view" of his misfortune and saying icily in turn that he had found it impossible to reply any earlier. "All my friends, including philistine acquaintances, have on this occasion . . . given me proof of greater sympathy and friendship than I could have looked for." On 24 January Marx replied, after allowing "some time to elapse," saying that he had been very wrong to write as he had done. He had been "shattered" when the original letter had arrived, but the events of the day had made him desperate, as the family had been "in the same plight as the Manchester workers." On the twenty-sixth Engels replied, patching things up. Having extracted what he considered to be the appropriate emotional response to Mary's death, he wrote:

> Thank you for being so candid. You yourself have now realized what sort of impression your last letter but one had made on me. One can't live with a woman for years on end without being fearfully affected by her death. I felt as though with her I was burying the last vestige of my youth. . . . That letter, I tell you, obsessed me for a whole week; I couldn't get it out of my head. Never mind. Your last letter made up for it and I'm glad that, in losing Mary, I didn't also lose my oldest and best friend.

Engels's treatment of his dependents—the Burnses and the Marxes—was indeed self-sacrificing and generous. But there is an air of egocentricity and condescension in his account of his relationship with Mary, since he rather implied that her life was wrapped up in loving him. Indeed, hardly anything is known about her and their relationship other than his own brief testimony in the letters that survive. Even there he never said anything of substance or interest to his correspondents, so it is not surprising that they made little response save a few formal inquiries. Only in the case of her death was this pattern broken, and then Engels construed it exclusively as an event in his own emotional life, not something that affected anyone else, even her sister Lizzie who had discovered the body. Mary's own voice is unheard in the historical record, and there are no photographs or other likenesses of her, as there were at the time for virtually everyone else in these circles, even the servant Helene Demuth (Marcus 1974, 98–101; McLellan 1973, 331–332; Raddatz 1978, 148).

Engels: Domesticity and Marriage

"Mrs. Lizzy" fared somewhat better than Mary, and she at least was photographed. Possibly the image that survives is the one that Engels described in 1868 as awful but the least bad of five. The "Mrs." was again honorific, though it went with Burns, not with Engels. She resided, as before, at his private address, not his "official dwelling"—as Marx put it. Marx carefully sent his family's greetings to Engels, and his own to Mrs. Lizzy, in a letter of 5 August 1865, and on 9 August he reported that he had been severely cross-examined by his girls about this Mrs. Burns. He solicitously sought Engels to persuade her into membership of the International Working Men's Association, then just starting up in early 1865, as "ladies are admitted," and he hoped that she would follow her namesake the poet in thinking "a man's a man for all that" (Marx and Engels 1976–, 42:67, 91, 177, 181, 193; Marx and Engels 1956–1968, 32:182; 34: 336–337).

In the Marx-Engels correspondence, Mrs. Lizzy emerges—indirectly of course—as a considerable character. Like Mary, she did not meet the extended Engels family. In the summer of 1867 Engels planned to take her with him to the Continent, mentioning sights in Denmark and north Germany but proposing to send her home by way of Grimsby before he journeyed himself "to the Rhine"—where the Engels clan resided. As Marx's daughters were growing into young women, and as his family's circumstances improved somewhat when Engels's income began to rise, social relations between the two households increased, particularly when Eleanor visited Manchester and acquired fervent Fenian sympathies. These were nourished on trips to Ireland with Engels and Mrs. Burns. A letter from Eleanor to her older sister, Jenny, gives a fourteen-year-old girl's view of the Engels household in July 1869.

> On Saturday it was so warm that we, that is Auntie [Lizzie] and myself and Sarah [Parker—the maid], lay down on the floor the whole day drinking beer, claret, etc. . . . In the evening when Uncle [Engels] came home he found Auntie, me, and [Mary] Ellen [Burns—born ca. 1860, Lizzie's niece], who was telling us Irish tales, all lying our full length on the floor, with no stays, no boots, and one petticoat and a cotton dress on, and that was all [*Family Correspondence* 1984, 51–52].

Lizzie was considered a suitable companion for the Marx girls, and they occasionally spent time at the seaside together. Much of the correspondence that survives is about the lung complaints and other ill-health for which the sea air was considered beneficial, no doubt rightly in view of the notoriously polluted air in London. On Engels's retirement from business in June 1869 (at age forty-nine), he gave up his official dwelling and lived full-time with Lizzie in Manchester, but by early 1870 he was planning to move to London, saying that she had had words with her relations and did not wish to stay (Marx and Engels 1956–1968, 32:453).

Engels could hardly have wanted to remain in Manchester, so this development was obviously convenient, and a new domestic establishment—Engels, Mrs. Lizzie, Mary Ellen, and their maid, Sarah—was set up in September in the salubrious Regent's Park Road. Marx's wife, Jenny, had located the spacious house for them, commenting that "all round in the sidestreets there are shops of various kinds, so that your wife can look after everything herself." The two—Jenny Marx and Lizzie Burns—treated their ills together at resorts such as Shanklin and Ramsgate, and Engels fortified them on their "cures" with glasses of port (Marx and Engels 1956–1968, 32:714; 33:281; 34:26; Kapp 1972–1976, 1:183–184).

By the 1870s, Lizzie was "Mrs. E" in Engels's correspondence with Marx's daughter Jenny, but to his foreign correspondents she was Miss Burns of the Regent's Park Road, so that his name would not be linked with anything politically suspect. In the autumn of 1875 Engels and Lizzie journeyed through Germany to place Mary Ellen (known as Pumps) in a finishing establishment in Heidelberg—again bypassing the Engels clan. To his German correspondents, Lizzie was "my wife," though not in a letter to his brother Rudolf, in which Engels reported on his trip in a rather mysterious first person plural (Marx and Engels 1956–1968, 33:320, 417, 633; 34:164, 166).

Engels was always genuinely solicitous about Lizzie's health, taking her to Brighton in 1877, as she was continually ailing. Pumps was recalled early from Heidelberg to help with the household, as there had been all manner of trouble with maids, and Engels's efforts to make beds and light kitchen fires were laughable, so he said. By 30 July 1878 he pronounced Lizzie's condition very serious and feared the worst. She died on 12 September 1878, and Engels wrote at once to his brother Rudolf in Barmen of the death of his wife, saying that he had legally married Lizzie the previous evening. This is presumed to have been her deathbed wish, and the couple were married by special license. The marriage was performed by the local vicar, though Lizzie was buried in a Roman Catholic cemetery. Whether her aim was to be right with the world or right with God is unclear, but from Engels's point of view there could be little scandal or bad feeling in Barmen about the match. The new Frau Engels—already the late Frau Engels—would have no claim on the family socially and no chance of inheriting Friedrich's estate. It is difficult to escape the supposition that Lizzie might have preferred marriage at an earlier date and was refused it by Engels, who wished to keep his family affairs in order (Marx and Engels 1956–1968, 34:252, 255, 336, 342; Kapp 1972–1976, 1:184–192).

Engels: Widowerhood and Celibacy

A few days later, Marx recounted to his wife certain events at the Engels residence, retailed to him by Eleanor. This concerned the discovery of a small bundle of letters among Lizzie's things, and Marx commented that the scene was reminiscent of Balzac and the sentimental novelist Paul de Kock. Engels is supposed to have ordered the letters burned, saying melodramatically, "I need not see her letters. I know she was unable to deceive me." Mrs. Lydia Renshaw, a relation of Pumps, was in attendance and said later to Eleanor, "Of course, as he had to write her letters, and to read to her the letters she received, he might feel quite sure that these letters contained no secrets for him—but, they might do so, for her" (Marx and Engels 1956–1968, 34:344).

After the death of Mrs. Lizzie, Engels settled into what seems to have been a celibate widowerhood, looked after by a succession of female housekeepers and unnamed maids. These were Pumps at first, followed by Helene Demuth (Lenchen), who needed a situation after Marx's death in 1883, and, after her death in 1890, the divorced wife of Karl Kautsky, Louise née Strasser (see pp. 83–84, 93). As with so many other aspects of Engels's life, his later years merely marked the continuing pattern of his earlier ones—without the fire and enthusiasm.

Engels: Gender Power/Class Power

In his pursuit of conventional heterosexual masculinity, Engels does not seem to have gone searching for a relationship with any pretension to intellectual and moral equality. Rather, he seems to have sought political and domestic compatibility, both private pursuits by comparison with the public life he led as son and heir in the family business and in his other, semiclandestine life as a communist. Throughout his life he was strongly associated with the Barmen clan, through affection as well as necessity, and significantly he did not marry in the usual way and start his own family independently, as that would have cut him off altogether. His retirement allowed him to live openly with Lizzie Burns, as he had not been able to do with Mary. This was because he did not have business contacts to keep up, and because he had a politically sympathetic social life available in London, so he did not need diversions with the "philistines" of Manchester, among whom he had had genuine male friends. But there was little that was overtly unconventional in his arrangements in Manchester or London, as they corresponded closely to the way cross-class liaisons were handled in the mid-nineteenth century—the second household in the suburbs, the housekeeper who was not quite a wife. Later in life he said that he preferred Irish girls far above any bluestocking with social pretensions. While no doubt a true comment on his tastes, the remark is consistent with his general attitude toward women (Marx and Engels 1956–1968, 38:298).

Unless conceptualized by the biographer within a suitable frame—here, masculinity, gender politics, and sexuality—most of Engels's real life, as reconstructed from what might seem to be chance remarks, rare observations, and occasional personal events, simply disappears. Or if these matters do appear, it is only in a marginalized and somewhat prurient way. Now that the personal is political, there is every reason to explore what connections there were, or can be made, between the way a biographical subject conducted personal politics and public politics. Feminist theory and history provide the impetus to focus on a male subject's relationships with women (not just romantic involvements), and gender theory and history prompt an exploration of masculinity/ies and sexuality/ies (not excluding their conjunction with social class).

Conclusion

No matter how resolutely the subject's reputation is inscribed in the narrative tradition for certain great books or significant acts or influential thoughts, there is always the possibility of a radical reassessment. Indeed, I would suggest that received interpretative traditions should be changed for the sake of it. As biographers are necessarily different people, and as their situations are inevitably different, there is little point in successive biographers reproducing the same biography. In a short story, Jorge Luis Borges (1987) invents an author who rewrites certain chapters of *Don Quixote* exactly matching the text of Cervantes, not from an imaginative recreation of the sixteenth century, but from twentieth-century experience itself. Borges presumes that this exercise would require an immense exercise of concentration and intellect. Actually, I think that a number of biographers and commentators manage this feat of reproducing earlier biographies with relatively little difficulty.

Taking a lifeworld approach to biography dealing with a male subject is bound to make many more women visible in the narrative. This happens when space and time are reinvented as they must have been, rather than as they appear in the archival remains from which biographers normally work. While mothers have loomed large in biographical accounts (even in the lives of political theorists), female servants, siblings, other female relations, and eventually sexual attachments and liaisons will occupy more space and attention once the subject's experience enters the organizing structure of the narrative—qualified, of course, by actual context and available sources. This makes the subject a rather different character, that is, not just an author of books and pamphlets, but an author of power relations, as his sex and sexuality are lived out in the biographer's reconstruction.

Moreover, this approach tends to break down the traditional privileging of the public over the private, and to produce two texts: a narrative of domestic politics and one of public politics. It also makes it more difficult for the biographer to be complicit with the subject's own construction of public politics, as the masculinized character of the subject's practical and

theoretical assumptions will be made visible. This is because women necessarily appear in private life in ways that emphasize sexual difference, whereas in public texts and practices they often do not appear at all, or do not
appear in ways that make obvious the assumptions and practices attached to
femaleness.

Further, the lifeworld approach to biography actually raises and
resolves questions that might not otherwise be put to a text in political theory. These could be questions about men in reproductive activity and domestic circumstances, the persistence of gender hierarchies in pre- and postrev-
olutionary societies, the practice of dividing life metaphorically into public
and private spheres, the unexamined distinction between the politically significant and the merely personal. Wider, intergenerational issues may very
well arise, as they did with Engels, whose continuing relationships with parents and siblings, and presumed refusal to procreate, provide a curious coun-
terpoint to his reproductively centered account of the nuclear family in several classic texts—*The German Ideology,* the *Communist Manifesto,* and
The Origin of the Family (Marx and Engels 1970, 43–44, 48–50; 1980,
49–50, 466–509). Paradoxically, the ties of the bourgeois family, which he
excoriated as hypocritical and inhumane, trumped the political solidarity
and egalitarian sexual relationships that he advocated when he discussed the
proletarian present and the socialist future. Keeping mistresses in the suburbs and marrying on a spouse's deathbed conform to just the sort of bourgeois claptrap of which the *Manifesto* complains. The argument that Engels
made himself a willing victim to these disadvantages in order to finance the
Marx family through their undoubted tribulations falls victim to the further
consideration that Engels's attachment to Marx was in some respects itself a
relationship within dominant masculinity that trumped all the above. This is
not to say that the intellectual and political relationship that Engels formed
with Marx (and then carefully reformed in print after Marx's death) is other
than completely genuine in intellectual and political terms. But there is also
an element of hero-worship and unbalanced affection that is a recognizable
aspect of gender relations between heterosexual men. The epistolary tiff
after Mary Burns's death was perhaps an occasion when suppressed feelings
were allowed to come out.

Engels had no wish to join the proletariat by breaking with his family,
either by making the Burns sisters "respectable" (seriatim) or by breaking
off with the communist Marx. Thus, Engels had two public lives (as an
industrialist and as a communist) and one private one (as a lover of working-class women). But it was the public (albeit clandestine) life with Marx
(when alive and when dead) that clearly occupied his best efforts and atten-
tions in order to serve another, and the private one where he expected others
(female) to serve him. His family life (with parents and siblings) occupied
him least, though with the crucial intensity that the material necessities of

life are bound to inspire. These family members were almost always at a geographical remove, and unsurprisingly relationships across the generations do not figure much in his classic texts.

From our present perspective we are entitled to pick over the past, especially past lives, including their personal aspects. By looking behind our present political context, and by stepping outside it, we perceive options for the future. An unexamined present necessarily yields a future that is more of the same. Narrative traditions are among the nightmares that weigh on the brain of the living, as Marx commented in *The Eighteenth Brumaire of Louis Bonaparte* (Marx and Engels 1980, 96). In my view, biography too often succumbs to rigor mortis, and it is up to biographers to work harder to make it live.

Biographers could inspire a critical assessment of almost any issue, as any reasonable recovery of a life would raise matters of contemporary importance. This can be done in ways that merely reinforce received truths that are among the most efficacious props of current power structures, most particularly the prevailing assumptions around masculinity, gender, and sexuality. Or it can be done in ways that challenge those structures by questioning traditional conceptualizations. Biography is not a window on the past, but a political act in the present. Among these traditions are the contextualizing stories that accrete into a politics of interpretation, such as the episode I explore in Chapter 4.

In pursuing the way that narratives attach to political theorists, I shift my focus from biography as a genre to the biographers who actually construct the texts we read. My example is the story of Marx's illegitimate son, as it shows how contextualizing biographies are characteristically constructed from materials assembled within the gender politics of the biographer. Moreover, biographers themselves can be seduced away from scholarly standards by failing to notice that their factual narratives contain dramaturgical elements. Thus it is easy for dramaturgy to drive the narratives they construct, and for highly charged (but insufficiently evidenced) material to appear as fact.

Sometimes this controls what biographers have to say, and what their readers are supposed to think. Once such stories circulate there is little that can be done, as mud sticks, and deconstruction never wipes clean. However, I will make the effort to undermine one story in particular, if only to demonstrate that gender (ways that sex and sexuality become power relations in society) is a feature of intellectual communities, and not merely of the people that intellectuals write about.

4

Founding Fathers and Bastard Sons: Marx, Engels, and Freddy Demuth

Men's history—masculine history, if you will—begins when we redefine our usual notion of historical significance and when we shift our usual frame of reference. Once we have made these two conceptual adjustments, we uncover some secrets hidden in the familiar landscape of the past. More often—and ultimately more important—as we shift our angle of vision, we recognize new meanings in the evidence that lay in front of our eyes all along.

—Filene 1987, 104

Noncommunist biographical accounts of Marx, and similarly most of those of Engels, and even those of other figures in and around the Marx family and the political world of turn-of-the-century socialism, relate the tale of Freddy Demuth, "Marx's illegitimate son." Here we have a point where scholarly values in political theory, the revelatory perspectives of feminist theory, and the arguments from men's history can be made to converge. This is by way of introduction to the discussion that follows. However, my overarching argument concerns how narrative and genre have gripped the production of intellectual history and biographical representation within political theory itself, as encapsulated in the canon of great books by great thinkers. In a phrase, the story below moved from fiction to fact because it is a good story, not because it passes the tests of documentary evidence that scholars are meant to apply. Among those tests are questions of authenticity, authorship, chronology, selectivity, and plausibility. Examination of this "truth" about one of the great men in political theory requires reference back to surviving materials and reference forward to little-known lives. Most of all it requires some critical consideration of genre type and narrative within it, as long-lost letters, Victorian deathbed narrative, and gossipy tale-telling merge into myth, as we will see.

Filene (1987) argues that traditional history has indeed been mostly about men, but notably about what men do in public. Aside from "traumatic episodes" when "the public front collapses," private life and private activities stay private and off the historical record, except for "gestures" and "paragraphs here and there," when historians feel their narrative needs livening up. Filene's examples of major points in historiography when the public-private boundary is crossed in a notable way include the abdication of King Edward VIII "for the woman I love," when romantic and sexual feeling became an event in history, and President Franklin Roosevelt's polio and Randolph Churchill's syphilis, when contrasting narratives of the body took center stage. At these moments in historical dramaturgy the personal becomes historical, and historiography can, and usually does, become politicized. That is, any such narratives of sexuality, bodily disability, and affliction are easily moralized; more easily moralized—oddly, it might seem— than the kind of public events of which history usually consists. Traditions of value neutrality and Realpolitik secure the historian's place as chronicler of decisions, policies, peacekeeping, and war, which occupy some discursive space away from or over against the merely mundane, petty, and personal. When histories focus on the mundane, petty, and personal they are classed as salacious memoirs, scandalmongering, scurrilous testimony, and generally discounted as overmotivated and unreliable.

Nonetheless, we are thoroughly familiar with the chronicles of the contemporary press concerning sexuality and sleaze. While the press is more than capable of waiting, watching, spying, and entrapping its public victims as they lead their private lives, there are also disaffected associates, political enemies, and security services in the game, planting information, innuendo, and fiction anywhere in the media. Not all is sniping and disinformation, however, as haloed and hagiographical representations of the rich and famous, both dead and alive, are readily available. Representation, as with all communication, leaves meaning surplus to language, and lends itself not just to multiple and unpredictable interpretations, but to many-layered ambiguities and ironies (Seery 1990). Thus, we may enjoy our disapproval and even remark that it would be a dull world in which the public mighty were not privately naughty and opprobrious. We might even hypocritically idolize them the more, the worse they are. Have the revelations of callous and commercial sexuality, betrayal, and hypocrisy, even lurid sibling rivalry and alleged Mafia connections, done much to diminish the myth of John F. Kennedy and Camelot? The mythical element in Arthurian Camelot was the vision of moral purity and spotless rectitude among rulers, while the tale itself was driven by quite different motivations, much more like the ones we will meet below.

Story Telling

Frederick Demuth has become an important character in the history of political thought, and his existence is sometimes noted as if its significance were self-evident. Unlike most other aspects of the lives of Marx and Engels, which have been thoroughly turned over as a matter of course by intellectual biographers, Freddy is curiously underinterpreted, and his role undertheorized. Freddy would be an altogether minor character today, were it not for a document first published in extracts in 1962. According to the story recounted there, Freddy was a relation of Marx and his family and—in an ambiguous way—of Engels. Ostensibly, the tale concerns Marx and his supposed affair with the housemaid Helene Demuth, but it is Engels who plays the central role in the supposed narrative, though, as ever, the tendency among commentators to swing any narrative toward Marx is present.

The typewritten document has been accepted by some scholars as entirely genuine, but hotly disputed by others as a forgery, possibly by Nazi agents aiming to discredit socialism by denigrating socialists. It appears to be a letter dated 2/4 September 1898, written by Louise Freyberger née Strasser, three years after the Engels household broke up on Engels's death in 1895. As Louise Kautsky, she had been asked by Engels, within a month of Helene Demuth's death, to keep house for him, and she arrived posthaste from Vienna. In 1894 she married Dr. Ludwig Freyberger, another London émigré, and he came to live in Engels's house, too—much to the displeasure of Eleanor Marx (Marx's youngest daughter), as she disliked Louise and her influence over Engels, then in his seventies (Kapp 1972–1976, 2:444; Henderson 1976, 2:725–726).

Freyberger's purported letter spins a lurid tale of deathbed revelations by Engels to Eleanor, principally the claim that Marx himself was Freddy's father. Fearing gossip imputing paternity, Engels is said in the letter to have declared the truth, in case he should be accused, after his death, of treating Freddy shabbily. The date of the document is some six months after Eleanor's suicide, so if there had actually been a letter, Eleanor was conveniently out of the way, though others mentioned as in on the story to some degree—such as Sam Moore, Marx's English translator, and Eleanor's sister Laura—clearly were not. The addressee of the supposed letter, the prominent German socialist and trade unionist August Bebel, or anyone else who had been the recipient of such tales from Louise, could have checked with them. The Freyberger letter—if such it is—has put Marx, his works, and his politics into a scurrilous realm of hypocrisy, and made Engels's deathbed into high Victorian melodrama. After such a gothic story it is extraordinarily difficult to see the situation any other way, but this now well-known version of events must nonetheless be tested stringently against what else survives as historical record. The actions—attested and alleged—of everyone involved must be carefully scrutinized, and feminist theory/men's history provides useful guidelines.

In a biography of Marx, published in English translation in 1978, Raddatz quotes the purported letter from Louise Freyberger as follows:

I have it from General [Engels] himself that Freddy Demuth is Marx's son. Tussy [Eleanor Marx] pressed me so hard that I asked the old man direct. General was most surprised that Tussy should cling so persistently to her belief and authorized me then and there to deny the gossip that Freddy was his son should this be necessary. You will remember that I told you this long before General's death.

In addition, a few days before his death General confirmed to Mr. [Sam] Moore that Frederick Demuth was the son of Karl Marx and Helene Demuth; Moore thereupon went to Tussy in Orpington and told her. Tussy maintained that General was lying and that he himself had always said that he was the father. Moore returned from Orpington and urgently questioned General once more but the old man stuck to his assertion that Freddy was Marx's son and said to Moore: "Tussy wants to make an idol of her father."

On Sunday, the day before his death [on 5 August 1895], General himself wrote it down for Tussy on a slate [as he had cancer of the throat] and Tussy came out so shattered that she forgot all her hatred for me and wept bitterly with her arms round my neck.

General authorized us (Mr. Moore, Ludwig [Freyberger] and myself) to make use of this information only if he should be accused of having treated Freddy shabbily; he said that he did not wish his name to be besmirched, particularly when it would do no one any good. He had stood in for Marx in order to save him from a serious domestic quarrel. Apart from us and Mr. Moore I think that of the Marx children only Laura suspected the story, though she may not have had direct knowledge of it; [Friedrich] Lessner [an old '48-er] and the pawnbroker [?] also knew that a Marx son existed. After Freddy's letters [?] came to light Lessner said to me: "Freddy is in fact Tussy's brother; we were sure of it but could never find out where the boy had been brought up."

Freddy looks like Marx and it is mere blind prejudice to try and see some similarity to General in that typically Jewish face with its long blue-black hair. I have seen the letter which Marx wrote to General in Manchester at the time [see below, p. 95]; General was then not yet living in London but I believe that he had this letter but, like so much of their correspondence, has destroyed it.

That is all I know about the affair; Freddy has never learnt who his father was, either from his mother or from General . . . [Raddatz's ellipsis].

For Marx separation from his wife, who was terribly jealous, was always before his eyes; he did not love the boy; he did not dare do anything for him—the scandal would have been too great. He was sent as a paying guest to a Mrs. Louis (I think that is how she writes her name) and he took his name too from his foster mother and adopted the name Demuth only after Nimm's *[sic]* death [Helene was known as Nim or Nimmy]. Tussy knew perfectly well that Frau Marx once ran away from her husband in London and went to Germany and that Marx and his wife did not sleep together for years; it did not suit her, however, to give the real reason; she idolized her father and would concoct the most beautiful myths [Raddatz 1978, 135–136].

Raddatz is at least highly skeptical concerning the truth values in this narrative at every point and caustic about the discoverer of the document, the scholar Werner Blumenberg. Blumenberg claimed that around 1900 all the socialist leaders knew that Marx was Freddy's father, and Raddatz notes rightly that there is no evidence for this. Ultimately, however, Raddatz is agnostic, concluding that no one can know the truth now, and that this tale of imputed and reputed paternity will retain its status as a mystery (1978, 134–138).

Other biographers have been much less reticent and have simply recounted it in a factual mode. Singer (1980, 6) provides the briefest note and the least comment: "Jenny's [Mrs. Marx's] maid, Helene Demuth, still lived with the family, as she was to do until Marx's death. (She was also the mother of Marx's illegitimate son, Frederick, who was born in 1851; to avoid scandal, the boy was raised by foster parents.)" The apparently feminist framing of the tale around motherhood in Singer's text is probably unintentional, as in the rest of the biography the focus is firmly on life and love as traditional history would have them—as addenda or footnotes.

This is also true in Berlin's (1978) well-known biography of Marx. He incorporates the tale in a footnote about Lenchen Demuth, "to whom Marx became attached." About Freddy, Berlin notes that Marx did not appear to like him, and that he was looked after by "the faithful Engels." Freddy, he says, "was a manual worker, and appears to have died at the age of eighty [actually seventy-seven] in England [London]" (p. 145).

In an illustrated biography, Blumenberg (1972) presents his discovery in the context of the Marxes' marriage. He gives a general treatment of the relationship but anchors this chronologically in the 1850s, when their domestic misery and wretchedness were extreme. He implies that Marx had added this "personal conflict" to an already intolerable situation and states that "Marx and his wife" were "thoroughly bourgeois" in their actions and thoughts—and hypocrisies. In a curious flight of fancy Blumenberg then compares Marx with Dickens (an "amorous double life") and Beethoven (fathering "a daughter by one of his admirers"), concluding that Marx should rise in our estimation because he transcended the conflicts around him, "which would have destroyed weaker personalities far more quickly" (pp. 122–126).

McLellan, in his life of Marx (1973), again locates the tale in the miserable 1850s, but in the context of his comments on Mrs. Jenny Marx and an excerpt from her (short) autobiography: "In the early summer of 1851 an event occurred that I do not wish to relate here in detail." While this might refer to any number of things, it does not seem implausible to take it to mean Freddy's birth, though McLellan attaches Marx's paternity to Freddy at that point in his narrative as a matter of fact. The reader is then guided through the purported Freyberger account, and McLellan states, "There is no doubt of the general credibility of this letter." Following that, he quotes some lines from Marx's correspondence concerning "unspeakable infamies," talebearing and tactless people, though there are no specifics and the assumption in McLellan's narrative is that this relates to allegations concerning Marx's ménage (pp. 271–273; see below, pp. 89, 94).

Engels's biographer Henderson (1976, 726–727) presents the story as a "distressing" episode disturbing Engels's final illness and otherwise peaceful deathbed in 1895, but he does not comment on how or whether Engels "accepted paternity" during the previous years, as the Freyberger letter states. Nor does he comment on whether the alleged change of mind on this question is plausible, not to mention any difficulties with the authenticity of the document itself.

Kapp (1972–1976), by contrast, treats Freddy sympathetically and extensively as the half brother of her subject, Eleanor Marx, and presents the few additional things that are known about his life till it ended in 1929. She has no difficulties with the document that Blumenberg says he discovered in 1962, indeed taking its authenticity as unquestionable in virtue of his status as a scholar, but she expresses considerable misgivings about Louise Freyberger and her (presumed) account of matters to do with the Marx family. Claiming that Louise wrote "in a vein of high fantasy," Kapp reviews all Freyberger's claims in the light of what is otherwise a matter of record, and is particularly good on the allegations concerning what various parties could certainly have known and what they were so confidently said to have destroyed. Kapp concludes that the Freyberger letter gives

> a distorted picture of the Marx family relationships and, in particular, shows Eleanor in a false light, while stamping Louise Freyberger as an unreliable and destructive person of coarse mind who waited four years— when Eleanor had been safely dead for six months—to betray Engels's trust [v. 1, pp. 296–297].

Extraordinarily, though, Kapp goes on to say that not all of Freyberger's account should be dismissed—just everything except two "facts": "Marx was Frederick Demuth's father," and "Engels informed [Eleanor]." Quite why these and only these data are assumed salvageable from Louise Freyberger's "vulgar twaddle" (Kapp's phrase) is not explained, save for a nonevent, namely that "no ugly gossip" bringing Engels or Marx into disrepute surfaced till the "scavengers of the future" got hold of Louise's letter. Finishing her discussion, Kapp takes the Blumenberg line that historical importance is not diminished by scandal (at least of this type, apparently), and that Freddy's real place in history is as Eleanor's most loyal friend during the psychological depression and bitter despair leading to her suicide in 1898 (v. 1, pp. 294–297).

Barrett (1983) locates the tale within an evaluation of the comparative worth of Marx and Engels to the feminist cause, as she construes it, and particularly to the practical matter of making problematic "the familial and sexual arrangements" that are considered normal and generally taken for granted. On this score she finds Engels's work "more modern" on the subject of women's oppression, and his approach to "personal relationships" through utopian socialism more flexible than Marx's. She takes the Freddy Demuth episode to be crucial to her negative evaluation of Marx with respect to the well-known feminist claim that the personal is political and to a further demand (which she thinks is feminist) that revolutionaries practice what they preach.

Barrett follows closely Kapp's acceptance of the authenticity of the document and gives selective credence to Freyberger's claims, notably restating that Marx "fathered Frederick Demuth." This is in itself a rather narrow view of fatherhood, even compared with the terms of the Freyberger letter. Whether or not Engels made anything politically problematic in his supposed acceptance of paternity during Marx's lifetime, or indeed in any of his other personal relationships (see pp. 66–77), is not discussed. Nor are a myriad of other issues in gender politics mentioned in Barrett's account, such as the ones that I have raised so far. Barrett acknowledges that the "random examples" in which she deals are "somewhat unfair and can be misleading," but disingenuously notes that "they illustrate the point" she is making, which is that in her selective trawl through the Marx and Engels papers, she "suspects" that Engels commits fewer "howlers" in terms of her version of feminism than does Marx (pp. 214–217). This is, of course, one way of doing the politics of interpretation, though not one I would recommend.

Deconstructing Freddy

Let us refigure the story and take it up at the point where the first mention of Freddy occurs in documents arising from and contemporary with the lives of the principal characters (rather than the first documentation of Freddy himself, which is his birth certificate of 1851). Our source is the surviving correspondence of the Marx sisters—Jenny, Laura, and Eleanor. Jenny wrote to Laura in 1882 about a debt to Freddy and her inability to help Nim make a journey to Germany. Shortly after Freddy's mother died in 1890, Eleanor wrote to Laura, mentioning past wrongs and a sense of guilt.

> Freddy has behaved admirably in all respects and Engels's irritation against him is as unfair as it is comprehensible. We should none of us like to meet our pasts, I guess, in flesh and blood. I know I always meet Freddy with a sense of guilt and wrong done. The life of that man! To hear him tell of it all is a misery and shame to me.

In the next few years Eleanor, Laura, and their brother-in-law Charles Longuet helped Freddy out financially, and in 1892 Eleanor wrote to Laura:

> It may be that I am very "sentimental"—but I can't help feeling that Freddy has had great injustice all through his life. Is it not wonderful when you come to look things squarely in the face, how rarely we seem to practice all the fine things we preach—to others?

Engels did not mention Freddy in his will of 29 July 1893, in which there were numerous bequests, even to Pumps—though her share was cut down from £3,000 to £2,230 in a codicil of 26 July 1895, as she had perhaps had her eye too obviously on Engels's estate. Eleanor and Laura were asked by Engels in a letter to hold one-third (some £3,000) of their combined share in trust for Jenny Longuet's French children, who could not be named for legal reasons. The two women, in conjunction with their brother-in-law Charles, managed to channel some of the funds from Engels's estate to Freddy, as he was in financial difficulties. In late 1897 and early 1898—just before she apparently committed suicide—Eleanor was in a terrible state about money, her relationship with the philandering socialist Edward Aveling, and his deteriorating health. She wrote a series of moving letters, confiding in Freddy as Lenchen's son: "I don't think you and I have been very wicked people—and yet, dear Freddy, it does seem as if we get all the punishment." "I say to you what I would not say to anyone now," she continued, "I would have told my dear old Nymmy *[sic],* but as I have not, I have only you" (Kapp 1972–1976, 2:680–688; Henderson 1976, 2:727–730; *Family Correspondence* 1984, 224, 240, 285; Marx and Engels 1956–1968, 39:318–319).

It is not apparent from the reliable evidence that survives exactly what injustices Eleanor thought Freddy had suffered and at whose hands. None of the Marx girls seemed at all preoccupied with paternity in their dealings with Freddy, and all three accepted him as Lenchen's son. How long they had known of his existence and his maternity (as it were) is not known. Possibly they were troubled about him and inclined to thoughts of guilt because he had grown up apart from his mother, so far as is known, and had enjoyed few educational advantages. Any feelings that his mother had been disadvantaged did not occur to them or at least did not surface in the correspondence that survives. Children were commonly put out to nurse in the 1850s, even among poor families like the Marxes, whose little Franziska (28 March 1851–14 April 1852) was boarded out at about the same time as the infant Freddy.

Or so we must presume, as Freddy never turns up in any materials from within or outside the Marx family until the letter of 1882 quoted above. Mrs. Marx gave this account in her memoirs written in 1865: "We gave the poor little thing [Franziska] to a nurse, for we could not rear her with the [three] others [Edgar, who did not survive, and Jenny and Laura, who did] in three small rooms." Lenchen, then about six months pregnant, was obviously in much the same position, except that housemaids who became pregnant were lucky to be kept on. Then, in her memoirs, Mrs. Marx also referred to the event "in the early summer of 1851"—Freddy was born on 23 June—that caused them much distress, but gave no specifics. As McLellan (1973) notes, Marx's letters of the following August speak of infamies and tales, but unlike McLellan, Marx named names:

> My wife will go under if things continue like this much longer. The con-
> stant worries, the slightest everyday struggle wears her out; and on top of
> that, there are the infamies of my opponents . . . who seek to avenge their
> impotence by casting suspicions on my civil character and by disseminat-
> ing the most unspeakable infamies about me. Willich, Schapper, Ruge and
> countless other democratic rabble make this their business [Marx and
> Engels 1976–, 38:402–403].

The context here is probably the breakup of the émigré German communists after 1848–1849 into rival groups who quarrelled bitterly about money as well as politics.

More pertinently, Marx had written to Engels on 31 March 1851 about a "mystery"—"in which you also figure"—that had given matters a "tragi-comic turn" [Marx and Engels 1976–, 38:324–325]. But in writing that letter he was interrupted, and in his following letter, 2 April, he put off relating the matter to Engels until his visit to Manchester at the end of the month. One possibility here was political intrigue. From mid-1850 the Prussian ambassador in London, and the Prussian government itself, had been conducting a campaign to discredit Marx and Engels and other communists, and in March 1851 Ferdinand von Westphalen, stepbrother of Mrs. Marx and a Prussian civil servant in the Ministry of the Interior, was involved in moves to secure the deportation of the chief revolutionaries from Britain. Prussian methods included the use of agents to find compromising material and to collect rumors and allegations that might influence the British government to comply with plans to push the communists further afield, and Marx and Engels were circumspect in their correspondence [Marx and Engels 1976–, 38:626–627 n. 454].

But it may alternatively have been the case that the housemaid's pregnancy was under discussion. Engels, who was supporting the Marxes on his slender resources, was in a position to pay to have the infant fostered, but there is no record of any arrangements to which he may or may not have willingly agreed.

If any of the odd comments in letters and memoirs were really about the pregnant Lenchen and her infant offspring, then the affair seems to have been viewed as an inconvenient embarrassment by Marx and as a source of personal distress by his wife, but there is no sense that Marx was intimately implicated as a husband and father, nor that Mrs. Marx saw him any differently, nor that Engels was going to be seriously put out as a friend, because the comments that do survive indicate that everyone involved was on much the same terms as usual. The pregnant housemaid and the problem of her baby were real—but evidently peripheral to the domestic difficulties with money and political difficulties with spies and communists that the Marxes and Engels had to endure during this period (Raddatz 1978, 23–24; McLellan 1973, 271–273).

At the time of Freddy's conception in 1850 and birth in 1851 the four principals in the affair, so far as we know, were Lenchen, Marx, Mrs. Marx, and Engels. The birth of an illegitimate child to the maid was obviously difficult and trying for the household, because the situation precluded any truly humane solution. Mrs. Marx would not have wanted to lose her longtime maid, and Lenchen no doubt wished to keep her livelihood. Continued residence for Lenchen with the Marxes, together with her illegitimate baby, would have associated the household with "free love" and moral irresponsibility, whoever the father was in fact or by repute. This was especially problematic with respect to the legitimate children, who would have been confronted—according to the standards of the time—with an example of flagrantly immoral behavior, and one specially relevant to young girls. These were standards held by both conventional conservatives and responsible communists, albeit for somewhat different reasons.

The section of the *Communist Manifesto* (1848) in which the bourgeois family is criticized from a communist perspective still makes very interesting reading, especially in conjunction with the real families and relationships that existed around the authors of the text (Marx and Engels 1980, 50). In any event such an immoral establishment would have been poor publicity for communism, and a considerable burden for the children, both legitimate and illegitimate, to bear. Lenchen could have been set up outside the family with her baby, but this was probably—with or without genuine regrets—beyond Engels's means, and certainly beyond his wish to spare his own extended family the possibility of serious embarrassment, as his connection with immorality might well leak out, whether or not he was presumed to be the father. The Engels family were, in any case, his employers. The obvious solution was to board the child Freddy out and leave him there, and that is in fact what happened, so far as we know.

Lenchen may not have objected very much, as it was clearly for her own good to keep her situation, for the Marx family to continue unencumbered, and for the communist cause to suffer no invidious criticism. The fact that she continued in the household with evident aplomb accords both with this hypothesis and with Eleanor's evident blankness on any injustice done to

Freddy's mother, whose infant had gone to another home. The grievous injustice, from Eleanor's point of view, could well have been the fact that Freddy had to grow up as a foster child—no doubt a hard upbringing—away from his mother and the civilized influence of a cultured household, such as the Marxes maintained even in direst poverty.

Throughout their lives all four principals lived happily enough together, so far as we know, and Lenchen ultimately served in both the Marx and the Engels households without any suggestion of reluctance. Helene Demuth was the daughter of a Rhineland village baker, and at an early age she had become the young Jenny von Westphalen's maid at home. She joined the Marx family in their Brussels days in the mid-1840s in order to help look after the infants. From all accounts she was good-humored and literate, and in later years she helped the married daughters, Jenny and Laura, with their babies. After 1883 the Longuet children—Jenny's—were settled with their widower father, Charles, in France; the three children of Laura and Paul Lafargue had all died in childhood by the early 1870s. Lenchen ruled over the Engels household until her death at seventy in November 1890. Engels wrote to his old friend Friedrich Sorge, an émigré '48-er living in New Jersey, giving this tribute:

> My good, dear, faithful Lenchen died yesterday afternoon. . . . We have lived for seven happy years together here in this house. We were the last two of the pre-1848 old guard. . . . If Marx for many years, and myself in the last seven, found peace for our labours, it was basically her work. . . . I will sadly miss her wonderfully tactful advice on party affairs.

Engels spoke at her funeral, and she was buried with the Marx family. In her will she left everything—amounting to £95—to her son Frederick Lewis Demuth, born Henry Frederick according to his birth certificate, which named no father (McLellan 1973, 138; Kapp 1972–1976, 1:278–297, 2:429–440; Marx and Engels 1956–1968, 37:498).

Lenchen's is another unheard voice in history, as she left no written testimony other than her will, but memoirs of the two households attest to her willing service. If there were difficulties among the four principals in the 1850s—about finances, maternity, paternity, or whatever—they were swiftly settled and never revisited, according to the surviving correspondence and other papers. Mrs. Marx would hardly have remarked in her letter about disturbing events if she knew that Karl were the father, as she was most particular about the obligations of family life (as we know from her correspondence) and could not have wished to spread such a tale any further. Presumably she made her comments because they were about a situation—one that was outside her immediate relationship with her husband—that affected her deeply.

If Engels were the father, or had taken the rap for Karl, this story would surely have surfaced at some point in the émigré community, since spiteful gossips abounded. Indeed, Engels was quite capable of dishing up that sort of thing himself. Writing to Marx in 1846 about their communist contacts near Paris, Engels indulged himself in ribaldry: "The best of it is that in the house . . . there are 2 women, 2 men, several children, one of them dubious, and despite all this not a thing happens there. They don't even practice pederasty" (Marx and Engels 1976–, 38:55).

A considerable number of highly communicative people—not all of them lifelong friends of Marx or Engels by any means—knew, or could well have known, of Freddy's existence, and it seems to have been no particular secret that Freddy's mother was a close associate of both Marx and Engels. Had there ever been a serious possibility that Freddy's paternity would pose problems for either of the two—and hence for the Marx party within the communist movement—the principals could easily have passed him off as a Demuth nephew or other relation.

Freddy, who was thirty-nine when his mother died, was evidently well known to the Marx girls as Lenchen's son, as the correspondence quoted above clearly indicates. Indeed, the adult Freddy was known and loved in the family as Lenchen's son, who had suffered a great injustice and needed to be helped. Eleanor spoke of him in those terms before Engels's death and afterward, and for that reason she is unlikely to have been the recipient of revelations on the subject of Freddy and unlikely to have sorted the Engels papers to remove any proof of Marx's paternity. If she had learned in 1895 of something scandalous, she could hardly have gone on with Freddy exactly as before and made almost exactly the same kind of comments about injustice. The correspondence that survives concerning Freddy reflects a steady, continuing interest in him on the part of the Marx girls, and vice versa. This begins sometime before 1882 and continues up to his final correspondence with Laura, shortly before her suicide in 1911.

Insofar as Lenchen was a second mother to Eleanor, Freddy was a kind of half brother, and because Lenchen was in effect a member of the Marx family, Eleanor's efforts to put him on a par with the other Marx legatees of Engels's will are understandable in those terms alone. Also the Engels estate was probably her only source of spare cash. Eleanor commented quite correctly in 1892 that Freddy was part of Engels's past but did not mention the other three principals of the original affair, because by the time of her letter they were all dead. Later, when she mentioned again the injustices done to Freddy, she did not mention Engels, because by that time he was dead, too.

Engels's reported irritation with Freddy suggests that he did not want some old embarrassment exhumed, as there was no way that Freddy's circumstances could reflect well on himself and the Marxes as communists, and there were numerous ways that it could be construed to bring discredit on the movement. With Freddy on the scene in London, questions might arise about his treatment in early life or just possibly his paternity, and the difficult matter for Engels of proving himself or others innocent of all callous behavior might arise if such an ill-natured and unedifying inquiry were opened. But, of course, we do not know exactly what Eleanor may have meant.

Engels had already put himself up for criticism in respect of the Burns sisters, and so he was party already to conventional discretion as a first line of defense. His liaisons were never widely advertised, they were never made to look like free love, and they never involved children—though exactly why not, and how this was contrived, we do not know. Thus they appeared, to those who were determined to inquire, to be responsible domestic relationships that had merely forgone the formalities of marriage. As he was evidently doing right by the Irish girls, not too much could be made of his living arrangements by conservatives bent on gutter politics or communists with scores to settle against Marx. The situation with respect to Freddy might well have been more difficult to explain and less easy to justify.

Reconstructing the Family

The most curious thing about the Freyberger letter is that it contains allegations about Marx and Engels that are quite sensational, but until the 1960s quite unknown. The letter was addressed to one of the most prominent socialist leaders in Germany. Did it actually reach him, or did it go astray, or was it never sent? In any case, why did Louise never raise the matter again? She was nothing if not energetic and determined, and as the intention of the letter was plainly to impose a revelation on the world, it seems inconceivable that she put pen to paper once and then let the sensational story drop for no less than the *fifty-two years* that elapsed before her death in 1950. Other than the general espousals of trust and occasional points of criticism that feature in the accounts above, little attention is paid to Louise Freyberger as a person, with a life. How can this document be squared with the supposition that she was in possession of such information, but on one, and only one, occasion wrote a letter and never seemed to have noticed the nonresult?

The Freyberger letter is very probably inauthentic. Even if it were authentic, Louise's account of the deathbed revelation is as suspect as some of the other "facts" in the document. And even if the tale of Engels's deathbed were truly told, the validity of his claim that Marx was Freddy's father is open to doubt. Of the two, Engels himself was a better candidate for paternity than Karl, and he was indeed living in London at the relevant time, September–October 1850. The younger, unmarried, and handsomer man was the one with a taste for girls, working-class ones at that, and Lenchen was his exact contemporary. Writing to Marx from Paris in 1847, Engels let rip about grisettes—"easy" working-class girls named for their cheap gray attire.

> It is absolutely essential that you get out of boring Brussels for once and come to Paris, and I for my part have a great desire to go carousing with you. . . . If I had an income of 5,000 francs I would do nothing but work and amuse myself with women until I went to pieces. If there were no Frenchwomen, life wouldn't be worth living. But so long as there are *grisettes,* well and good! [Marx and Engels 1976–, 38:115]

By contrast, Karl was notably stuck on Jenny as his only love, and from all accounts he was uxorious in the home—even if he did complain a bit in letters to his best friend—and desperately anxious for a son. He mourned his two dead ones—Edgar or "Musch" (1847–1855) and Guido or "Föxchen" (1849–1850)—with particular bitterness. At a time when the younger boy had only recently died, in November 1850, and on the occasion of his third daughter Franziska's birth in March 1851, he commented, "My wife, alas, has been delivered of a girl, and not a boy. And what is worse, she's very poorly." When his last surviving child, Eleanor, was born in January 1855, he wrote to Engels, "my wife was delivered of a bona fide traveller—unfortunately of the 'sex' *par excellence.* If it had been a male child, well and good."

Lenchen and Mrs. Marx were very close—Lenchen was a link for Jenny with the von Westphalens and happier days—and Frau Marx was virtually all that Helene Demuth had in the world. The two no doubt spent more time together than Jenny spent with Karl, who devoted long hours to his work in the British Museum. It seems difficult to imagine Lenchen deceiving her mistress, and if violence were perpetrated on the maid by Karl, it seems difficult to imagine Jenny allowing the household to continue as if nothing had happened. Surely the maid would have had to go.

Jenny complained on occasion about August Willich, one of the expatriate '48-ers, saying that he was lurking around the household with seduction on his mind. Someone like that seems a better candidate for Freddy's father than either Marx or Engels. At registration, Freddy was named Henry, possibly after Karl Heinrich Marx, and Frederick, possibly after Friedrich Engels, who had no alternative Christian name but sometimes anglicized his own. The two men were very possibly charged by the unhappy mother and her distraught mistress with doing the best they could for the infant—with discretion and at a distance (Marx and Engels 1976–, 38:326, 39:509; Kapp 1972–1976, 1/21; McLellan 1973, 246–247).

The story of Marx's illegitimate son is the most obvious reading of the Freyberger letter, but the central player in the narrative is Engels, scratching away at his slate (so the resulting testimony could not survive?). Hence the tale should also be particularly scrutinized for its allegations about Engels, namely his behavior on his deathbed and before. In the letter Freyberger says,

> [Engels] said that he did not wish his name to be besmirched. . . . He had stood in for Marx in order to save him from a serious domestic quarrel. . . . I have seen the letter which Marx wrote to General in Manchester at the time. . . . I believe that he had this letter but, like so much of their correspondence, has destroyed it [Raddatz 1978, 134–138].

If Engels were genuinely worried at any stage that Freddy's paternity would be laid at his door—and there is no evidence that he was—he would hardly have wanted to destroy the one document that would have cleared him, as the Freyberger letter suggests. If, as seems more likely, he cared more for Marx's name within the communist cause than for his own respectability, then—if there were a letter incriminating Marx—he might well have burned it, but many years before Louise Freyberger arrived in his household in 1890.

However, there is little likelihood that on his deathbed Engels would suddenly demonstrate an overpowering concern for his own moral reputation in the shallowest sense, and then seek to salvage it from an entirely hypothetical attack by imputing Freddy's paternity to Marx. Indeed, Engels took special care to provide for the Marx children, and, if Freddy were one as well, he could easily have written another codicil and included him among the legatees. He would thus have protected himself from charges of shabby treatment with substantial help rather than with unsubstantiated allegations.

Overall, Engels was far more concerned for the good name of the communist movement, and for Marx's good name first and foremost within it, than he was for his own. By the time he died he had devoted fifty years to this cause, and he is unlikely to have wanted to blacken Marx's name for any reason whatsoever. The personal and the political were far too closely intertwined in his life to come apart so catastrophically; indeed they were virtually one and the same. The Freyberger letter illustrates precisely the kind of thing that he was least likely to say.

Conclusion

This chapter has allowed me to meditate on three themes that are not usually (or not yet) much considered within political theory and the commentaries on it. First, there is the relationship between a history of men—as the conventional history of what men do—and men's history—as a feminist-inspired study that makes the who, what, and where of history newly problematic. Thus, the private, the personal, and the domestic are reframed as historically central, rather than peripheral, trivial, or excluded. This opens a vast realm of subjects and concepts to direct scrutiny in political history, the history of ideas, and textual interpretation, all within a contextualizing narrative that is inevitably biographical. Many of the terms involved may seem familiar, as they are constitutive of ordinary life, whether then or now. But by the same token, they are not necessarily very well understood in the analytical sense. That is why a notion of gender linked to sex and sexuality can be useful in pushing political theory toward further areas in society where power relations bear more heavily on some than on others.

These terms include the negotiation of just outcomes in class-divided society, as witnessed above, in the various hypothetical, fictional, and documented accounts of how Engels's money was, was not, or might have been distributed among the second generation issuing from the Marx ménage. In a context marked by dominant heterosexual masculinities—ranging from the philandering to the uxorious—those masculinities are themselves further multiplied with respect to class; for example, alleged seductions of housemaids and grisettes (by a lifelong near bachelor concerned about inheritance), and morally respectable and procreative marriages (by a communist who had male offspring in mind). Arguably there are different sexualities at work here, in terms of reciprocal understandings and social meaning, rather than a constant and singular personal sexuality manifesting itself variously in different contexts and with respect to different objects. As another example, illegitimacy looms large in the particular case under consideration, not least because it concerned an actual person, but also because in documented respects, and in plausible terms, the Marxes were involved in negotiating a political representation of themselves as communists or socialists within a society in which inherited advantage and disadvantage was organized around an axis of legitimacy/bastardy, as well as around complex understandings of social class. In any credible study, this matter requires discussion, whereas in less-thoughtful accounts the term *illegitimate* is merely delivered to the reader unexamined, for its shock value.

Everyday relationships actually require continuous negotiation and achieve vast variety—I am thinking here of husband-wife, father and/or mother–child, friend-associate, and so on—and there is no reason to assign fewer capacities in this area to the subjects of a contextualizing discussion than we characteristically assign to ourselves, however different their personalities and circumstances are thought to have been. These negotiations within the Marx-Engels ménage are recorded—imperfectly, ambiguously, and selectively—in the archival materials that remain, and they need careful handling in some plausible account of the human relationships involved.

There are complex norms of, for example, reputation/guilt, fidelity/wild oats, and doing the right thing/different kinds of relationship, that operate within and behind the prose artifacts that remain for us. Exploration in these areas helps to mark the difference between persuasive contextualization and exploitative sensationalism, so I hope that my discussion of the Karl-Jenny, Jenny-Lenchen, Marx-Lenchen, Engels-Lenchen, Marx-Engels, Marx daughters–Lenchen/Freddy, and Engels-Freddy relationships lives up to this.

Second, I have demonstrated the appetite for biography among contextualizing commentators on the lives and thoughts of Marx, Engels, Eleanor Marx, and others. The gender politics of various commentators can be grouped, despite differences, into four broad categories: displacing, complicit, transcendent, and condemnatory. Raddatz is an agnostic about factuality, displacing judgment in respect of the Freyberger letter onto readers and leaving them with a mystery. Effectively this inscribes the story more firmly than ever in the record, as dramaturgically mystery is perhaps a more popular and pervasive form than tragedy. A suggestion that it might just lie alongside the relevant lives and works seems naïve. Allegations of mystery do not create an option to take it or leave it; an unresolved mystery is an invitation to the reader to become more involved in the telling of the story. Further retellings are incomplete without this important component. The gender politics here consists in simply serving up materials on their own terms and thus never engaging critically with the ways that sex and sexuality become power relations in society. If there were critical engagement, it would show up in the way the detailed materials were treated.

There are certainly many commentators who accept crucial parts of the Marx's-illegitimate-son narrative as factual record, and I have considered Singer, Berlin, McLellan, and Henderson. Exactly whom this story is about varies somewhat among and within the accounts, illustrating the protean quality that stories usually have once they enter the realm of interpretation. For Singer, Berlin, and McLellan, the story relates facts about Marx of which the reader should be aware, though they do not spend much time drawing out the supposed significance of the tale. Presumably, their view is that Marx was flawed as a moral agent, though intact as an intellect, but the relationship between text that functions as political practice and activities that issue from a political agent is only just noticed. The gender politics here is one of complicity, in that commonplace norms are covertly reinforced within the commentary. Indeed, the standards of consistency that commentators might apply in doing even this limited exploration are not well worked out in the first place. If the episode represents a lapse of character, is it also a political lapse in terms of Marx's writing on the hypocrisy of the bourgeois family, the call for a higher form of the family and of relations between the sexes, and the very moving passages in *Capital* on the exploitation of women and children (Marx and Engels 1980, 49–50; Marx 1986, 517, 620–621, 666 nn. 7–8, 724 n. 20)? How closely should Marx's character in terms of consistency be linked with a reading of his works as political prescription?

These are precisely the questions that the transcendental and condemnatory commentators raise in their accounts, though with the very different answers that my categorizations imply. Blumenberg and Kapp argue for a disjunction between character and politics, at least at the level of moral character and theoretical work, implying that greatness in the latter sphere overcomes whatever faults occur in the former. There are simply two Marxes in such an account: one with a body, an ordinary life, and all the difficulties of being a revolutionary in practice and/or by reputation; and another who participated in a transcendent realm of theory, abstraction, and truth. That realm is evidently supposed to be an effect of disembodied rationality and book-centered intellectualization, mental concentration that is or should be removed from quotidian anxieties and desires, and godlike participation in history making denied to the merely ordinary, for whom merely ordinary standards were invented. Yet this view then divorces texts in political theory, such as Marx's (or Engels's), from their status as contemporary politics, which was inevitably personal, detailed, and messy. This disjunction not only removes works from the lived experience of the author but also disconnects them from the author's intended illocutionary force in creating them as politics. However, because life experience and political experience are inseparable, behavior that is conventionally understood as moral is just as relevant as actions conventionally regarded as politically motivated. Both these things lie behind published works now recovered as political theory. Ultimately, commentators who argue transcendence drain the politics from political theory. While engaging with the larger issues that gender politics raises, they make their chosen subject exceptional by invoking what is in the final analysis a romantic account of genius and history.

Barrett is a theorist who argues for condemnation on precisely the opposite grounds. She states that the practice of revolutionaries should track their theoretical strictures. They should make problematic in their own practice what they theorize problematically, so theory and practice are necessarily linked, and similar criteria of judgment should apply. In both family relationships and the treatment of females, Marx is found badly wanting, and Engels is said to do somewhat better. The Freddy episode is an emblematic instance where this judgment is supposedly confirmed. This reading has the merit of dispensing with the crippling dichotomies into which the transcendence school necessarily falls, and also with a disingenuous move into historical relativism (their standards were appropriate at the time, and ours are inapplicably different) that might be made. It also rejects an overly simple division of the behavioral world into what is merely moral and what is excitingly political, or what is off-limits as personal and what is under consideration as public. But the disadvantage in Barrett's hands is her insensitivity to the conceptual complexities of gender (ways that sex and sexuality become political) within the further complexities of class, as she maps gender onto woman/women and ignores or misjudges the class boundary as Marx and Engels actually confronted it. This was negotiated by them at the time, both in terms of cash and in terms of status markers and gradations, such as illegitimacy, respectability, and obligation among friends, associates, employers, servants, and children. As I have tried to indicate in my own reading of the Freddy affair, there are also important relationships caught by the phrase *extended family,* as well as those covered by the rubric domesticity. Keeping this tangle manageably together in the present while behaving as the ideal communist of the future strikes me as an impossible conjunction to require, and in fact an invitation to view the subject as mad, or even an injunction to madness in actual behavior. On the other hand, I have argued that the intertextuality of political theory and lived experience is a real one, so interpretations are in order and judgments can be made. What is crucial is the process by which this is done.

For me, this involves not merely the insights of feminist theory/men's history, and an intuitive and imaginative process of reading through the panoply of concepts—including both personal ones to do with family relationships as well as public ones to do with socialist politics—but also the supposedly standard array of scholarly discriminations. In the case of Freddy Demuth, I argued that dramaturgy trumped scholarship too much of the time, and much of the apparatus I deploy in terms of detailed chronology, inclusive citation, multiple hypotheses, and straightforward skepticism is surely familiar to the commentators I cite. Yet, I have constructed this chapter as something of a meditation on the complicity that develops between scholarship and mythmaking, and in the end I am suggesting that simplistic myths are the worst. This is because they reinscribe the most commonplace categories and judgments within narratives that are influential precisely because they are framed as academic and reliable. The difficult matter of judging Marx's life and works—and the very business of trying to establish the terms on which this would be a useful exercise—is simply dumped there into a moralizing reaction to sexual scandal. But in whose or what terms is this scandalous? And what exactly licenses the commentator to dispense this judgment? Even if the smear or slight is mitigated by the desire to push it into the background as merely personal, it is bound to leak out once more into the public realm of theorizing about politics, where indeed it has become firmly lodged. One wonders how such commentators would react to an account of their own lives and thoughts constructed in such impoverished terms?

By now it should be apparent that class and sex interact in the above discussion in important ways, and that gender politics, in those circumstances, was crucially crosscut with class politics. But it could just as well have been religion, ethnicity, language use, or any other category of social exclusion. The extent to which this occurs has real effects on what can be meant by *woman* or *man*—or *gender* (the ways that sex and sexuality become power relations in society).

It should also be evident that attempts to contextualize a character who is (willingly or not) taken to be a political theorist is an activity closely related to the political and moral predilections of the commentator. Contextualization is essential to any reading of political theory; even a naïve reading reflects some contextualization, however minimal, as no reader is a tabula rasa. I contend that the contextualizations offered to us are affected not merely by surviving materials, selectivity, and tradition, but specifically by the commentator's appreciation of a good story, such as the one the Freyberger letter provides. Moreover, it seems to me that once a tale is attached, it is never detached: the mud will stick, and I cannot claim that my deconstruction will expunge the lurid mélange of genre that the letter contains. Yet, paradoxically, the story of Marx's illegitimate son has led to more productive readings of texts from life and life from texts than we ever would have had otherwise.

The politics of interpretation is itself practiced in ways that combine the themes covered in this chapter. Layered narratives incorporate the codefined categories of gender politics, class politics, race/ethnicity, and discursive power in yet other modes. In Chapter 5 I explore this process in a contemporary setting by shifting the focus once more, this time away from intellectuals and the academic arena, moving it toward politicians, officeholders and aspirants, the press and the public. This raises the issue of how popular culture enables political actors to function in a democratic society, and how a strategy of narrative multiplication can be used by men to disadvantage women.

5

"He Said/She Said": Interpreting the Clarence Thomas– Anita Hill Hearings

I think it's very interesting to listen to her because as I saw her there, she said it's a matter of interpretation. . . . ["]A long time ago this happened. I didn't do anything about it.["] . . . I don't say that it didn't happen but I'm convinced that there's another side to this story that says that it did not happen, at least in this manner, as this lady has put forward.

Q[uestion]. Senator, you're making a decision here based on accepting his credibility over her credibility.

A[nswer]. That's my job, yes, ma'am.

—New York Times, 8 October 1991

Every 15 minutes there was a new theory.

—Anita Hill, New York Times, 15 October 1991

Americans often say, "It's a matter of interpretation." This is true enough, but it is only recently that this insight has burst upon the social sciences, in what is known as the interpretative, or linguistic, turn. This, and a number of other important methodological moves, will be examined here before I turn to a reading of the Hill-Thomas hearings in order to explore further how perspectives, developed within feminist theory and gender theory, can usefully complicate our understanding of contemporary politics. In the course of this discussion, concepts of culture, race/ethnicity, identity, self, agency, participant, commentator, spectator, theorist, evidence, and event will all be rendered problematic. Paradoxically, perhaps, this will have the effect of drawing theorists and their subjects closer together in methodology and terminology. There will also be implications for theories of what democratic discourse is, and what it ought to be. Moreover, Hill-Thomas is a rare instance in politics when the activities of private man are not only out in public, but must perforce be taken seriously. Many male politicians found this extremely difficult to deal with personally—and politically.

Interpretation

The linguistic turn is a turn in methodology, and of necessity in basic assumptions. Specifically, it encompasses the claim that understanding arises out of textual interpretation, and that mechanistic or lawlike explanations of human behavior based on the supposed protocols of natural science are bogus (Bleicher 1980, 1981; Dallmayr 1987; Gibbons 1987; Shapiro 1986).

Behavior itself is invariably textualized when it is studied; data sets are actually texts, and have been shown to be embedded in broader narratives (Giddens 1982, 1987; for specific applications see, e.g., Ball 1987, on political science; Lavoie 1990, on economics; and Shanks and Tilley 1987, on archeology). Objects of interpretation that can be read as texts have successively expanded to include artifacts such as films or other images, and objects such as the human body or fossils (Boyne and Rattansi 1990; Haraway 1991). Further, deconstructionist or postmodern writers have successfully made problematic the notions of author and reader that interpretation requires (Murphy 1989; Ryan 1988). Moreover, illocutionary philosophies of language have evolved theories of performative utterance that locate understanding in a context of motivations and goals; "we understand differently when we understand at all" (Gadamer, quoted in Lavoie 1990, 2). Understanding takes place in a political context and is inevitably for some purpose or purposes, or functions as if it had such a purpose, and is inevitably interpreted within a purposive framework (Tully 1988). Of necessity this perspective extends to the interpreter or researcher, and I offer my own view of the utility of the present discussion at its close.

Culture

Culture can be conceptualized as a "complex convention" or compendium of "scripts" (Baudrillard 1988). Thus, ethnicity, gender, religion, language use, race, or whatever we (or they) wish to consider in terms of ascriptive and self-ascribed identities can be seen in the first instance as linguistic, rather than as biologically or historically hereditary; as conceptual material available for self-construction, self-interpretation, and self-presentation, rather than as conceptual reflections of some essential reality; as something we might theorize with, rather than theorize about; as something people do, rather than something they have to be (Martin 1991). These scripts can be explicated as "representations of sexual difference and identity which are in fact constructively imposed on human subjects." Characteristically, such constructions are "patterned in dualistic and hierarchical modes" that promote privilege and subordination. They are a ubiquitous feature of human society but have no "fixed transcultural or transhistorical meanings," and they are subject to constant reinterpretation by individuals and institutions (di Stefano 1991, 31).

This way of proceeding has the evident advantage (or hostage to fortune) of leveling out the various categories we consider relevant to culture. Thus, there is nothing more real or essential or fundamental about being a woman in a male-dominated society, or being black or of color in a white-dominated society, than in being a Catholic in a Protestant-dominated society or Finnish-speaking in Sweden. Some recent feminist writing has termed *woman* a category of oppression, rather than a reflection of biological difference, as it is the political presumption that a particular difference matters, and matters because it excludes, marginalizes, and demeans, which makes the category so efficacious for some and constraining for others (Ferguson 1984). The cultural universe is "elaborately carved and apportioned in terms of presumedly meaningful . . . differences" (di Stefano 1991, 31).

The cultural world is full of signs and markers that are used and read as signals; moreover, they acquire their full meaning as and when they are scripted into narratives, and narratives are applied in politics. Depending on the situation, language use or religion—which we might take to be acquired aspects of individuality rather than supposedly essential ones like ethnicity or sex—may be crucial. There is nothing that says that so-called obvious or inalterable or natural aspects of individuality are always and necessarily more important or fundamental just in themselves.

Race and ethnicity are not natural, even though they are often represented as if they were. Their boundaries are not fixed, nor is their membership uncontested. Race and ethnic groups, like nations, are imagined communities (Anderson 1991). They are ideological entities, made and changed in struggle, and the struggle is carried on in all manner of cultural media and contexts. They are discursive formations, signaling a language through which differences, which are accorded social significance, may be named and explained. They also carry with them material consequences for those who are included within, or excluded from, such groups.

Thus, identity is not simply imposed. It is also chosen and actively used, albeit within particular social contexts and constraints. Against dominant representations of others, there is resistance. Within structures of dominance, there is agency. Analyzing resistance and agency repoliticizes relations between collectivities and draws attention to the central constituting factor of power in social relations (Pettman 1991, 188–189, 191).

Moreover, this way of looking at culture democratizes in that it is in part left to individuals to self-categorize and to self-valorize such categorizations. This explains the amount of deviancy that we observe in opposition to stereotypical categorizations and valuations. But it is only categorizations of normality that establish deviancy and make it possible and visible. A linguistic perspective on culture points out the power of anarchocollective categorizations and institutional definitions in terms of policing, excluding, silencing, and marginalizing to keep the stereotypes in place and to maintain order in the political economy of cultural categories (Butler 1990).

Cultural categories may emphasize sameness at the expense of difference (whereas individuals may be more relevantly different, as they see themselves, within a supposed cultural group), or difference at the expense of sameness (whereas individuals may be more relevantly the same, as they see themselves, across a supposed cultural cleavage). Cultural categories may also de-emphasize individuality in favor of supposed collectivities, and de-emphasize what is discovered or invented individually in favor of what is given or enforced collectively (Connell 1987). Multicultural discourse—whether pluralist and based on interest, or ethnicist and based on essence—risks the dangers of categorial imperialism ("my interests are your interests") and dead-ending ("we are always going to be different from you") that feminists have already confronted (Martin 1991). As feminists confront women, so necessarily do men. In their categorial constructions of women they inscribe and reproduce cultural traditions, and so demonstrate very clearly how sex and sexuality become power relations in society (Zerilli 1994).

Having set out a characterization of culture and multicultural discourse, I move on to an example of cultural politics, noting how some of the signs and symbols familiar in U.S. politics were presented and read in new ways. I end with a speculative conclusion about narrative power as a mechanism through which politics is actually done. But in the discussion that follows I am also suggesting that the politics of class and gender interact here in two interesting and crucial ways: class is a subtext in U.S. politics, not often addressed, but usually invoked as race; and gender itself is not independent of cultural characterizations, but vastly complicated, indeed imbricated by them. Women of different races and in different classes are perhaps in different genders; certainly their gender politics is often different, and the ways in which others perceive them are often different (hooks 1982). They represent rather different ways in which sex and sexuality become power relations in society. Similar considerations apply to men, as we have seen earlier (see pp. 77–79) and shall see again.

Text

I take as my text for interpretative analysis the account of the Hill-Thomas hearings presented by the *New York Times* (hereafter NYT), from 7 to 20 October 1991. The *Times* is a newspaper of record with exceptionally full coverage, much verbatim material, a range of well-informed reporting, and far more reliability and insight than most journalism. Alternative or further studies could, and doubtless will, include the verbatim transcripts, video tapes from the various national networks that carried the hearings, radio tapes or transcripts of coverage, and other newspaper and journal accounts. I also make use of the *Washington Post* weekly edition, the *Wall Street Journal,* the *New York Review of Books,* and *Judicature,* but I strictly limit myself in the range of sources used for specific reasons, which are explained below.

Of course, in any study like this one, the amount of text or textlike materials expands toward the infinite, especially if polling or interviewing is considered. The *Times* includes a good deal of this type of material, as reporters were dispatched to a number of unlikely places to relate what "ordinary Americans" were thinking. The notion that the Hill-Thomas hearings were an event or series of events thus becomes problematic, as there are in a sense as many events as there are individuals who took some view about the participants and what they said. Because what participants said was politically charged all along, the circle of actual participants widened to include those in the various publics who might somehow register a reaction, most notably through opinion polls, congressional mail and telephone calls, and ultimately votes at the next election. Even for the *Times,* the event widened to include ordinary people as participants, not just onlookers, and the location of the event became somewhat indeterminate.

Thus, there is no neat way to frame participants or narrative (Scheppele 1989). The presumed distinctions among participants, spectators, and commentators swiftly dissolve into the conversational production of text: the typical *Times* reporter filed a story containing firsthand observation, quotation from major figures, comments from associates and bystanders, telephone interview and poll information, and a good-sized dollop of personal interpretative technique ranging from overtly radical feminism (Maureen Dowd) to traditional veteran reporting (R.W. Apple).

Everyone had his or her own Hill-Thomas hearings. But not all accounts are equally interesting nor is there any one authoritative version. The *Times* is an informative palimpsest to look at because it draws on so many sources and commands a loyal but critical audience. As an interlocutor for persuasive and transformative conversation in politics, it is better than most, though advertising this role would undermine the tropes, which are both reflected and subverted within reportorial discourse, that events happen out there, that reportage is not part of the facts, and that participants in an event should not include the press.

There can be little doubt that the Hill-Thomas hearings will be memorialized by political and cultural historians as a significant event, and indeed this process has begun (Morrison 1992). The U.S. Senate put itself through a uniquely contorted bout of self-criticism and self-defense; the TV audiences were enormous and other media coverage was extensive; parallels with historic events (notably the McCarthy hearings of the early 1950s) were swiftly established; and most important, the language was lurid and the drama intense. This was raunchy talk direct from the U.S. Capitol. It was courtroom drama with contradictory witnesses. It was sex, lies, and daytime TV.

Hypotheses

My hypotheses in doing this study are as follows. First, I presume that sexual, gendered, racial, and partisan politics were made to interact in new, complicated, and highly visible ways. Clarence Thomas was the black, Republican nominee for associate justice of the U.S. Supreme Court, filling a seat vacated by the first black man to hold that office, Thurgood Marshall. Anita Hill was a black, Republican law professor whose allegations suddenly disrupted the orderly process of confirmation. She claimed that Thomas had sexually harassed her when they had both worked at the Equal Employment Opportunities Commission, the federal agency responsible for implementing directives on sexual harassment. Hill accused the Democratic majority on the Senate Judiciary Committee assigned to review Thomas of not taking her allegations seriously because the committee was entirely male; the sole female (Republican) senator steadfastly supported Thomas.

To that hypothesis I add the view, derived from the *Times,* that class was also an issue, as both Hill and Thomas presented themselves as, and were viewed as, elite professional lawyers (both are graduates of Yale Law School), and therefore shared, or apparently shared, antisexist assumptions and equal opportunities rhetoric that working-class Americans, when interviewed, generally did not. Working-class narratives were strikingly different and were particularly hostile to Hill as a middle-class woman.

Second, I hypothesize that narrative analysis of analogy and metaphor in my text, that is, the *New York Times,* will reveal a set of interesting subtexts. I presume that Hill's calm references to "information" and "integrity," and Thomas's counterallegation that he was the "victim of a high-tech lynching," would be typical of presentational strategies adopted by any and all who could get media coverage. This could of course extend to dress, deportment, entourage, and general considerations of image making. While studies of these nondiscursive phenomena could be undertaken, I limit myself to their representation in the discourse of the *Times;* I do not attempt to use the discursive frame as a window through which to judge these things as they were actually performed.

I was particularly struck by two subtexts in the *Times.* One was the persistent construction of stories by various reporters around Manichaean dualisms and dramatic contradictions: the prim farm girl versus the cutthroat world of Washington careers; the hallowed halls of Congress versus raunchy language and locker-room talk; a full Senate vote as a decisive verdict on who was lying; reputations definitively on the line in each day's confrontations. This sports-page journalism seemed surprisingly old-fashioned after "Hill Street Blues," the U.S. television series of the early 1980s that left viewers with loose ends, story lines that never finished, and a general feeling of real-life anarchy.

Thomas will be forever scrutinized, on the bench and off it, in the light of his histrionic claims of ignorance, innocence, and integrity. Hill will probably continue to command respect as the woman who came forward courageously to challenge the male power structure. What happened to her will be interpreted as further reason for women to win public office. Indeed, this has already taken place, most prominently in a primary election upset in Illinois, where a black woman defeated an incumbent Democratic senator (Al "the Pal" Dixon) who had voted for Thomas (Abramson et al. 1992); it is also said that this phenomenon has peaked and that the effects will not be long-term.

The interpretation of political events is not as neatly dichotomous nor as make-or-break as the *Times* narrative suggested it was on the day. Perhaps among other things this is a device to move readers back the twelve to twenty-four hours that necessarily elapses between the time the paper reaches its readership and the time the events, as constructed, took place.

The other subtext was the overwhelming persistence of consistency as the sole and ultimate test of credibility, when, as the Federal Bureau of Investigation (FBI) put it, the case was of the "he said, she said" variety (note the sexual transposition). Throughout the *Times* narrative the supposition that the truthful individual is consistent, not just in stating and defending a truth, but in all aspects of behavior alleged to be relevant, reigned supreme. Hill suffered particularly for her decision to move to another federal agency in Washington, thereby presumably consenting to work with Thomas again, after the alleged harassment. Thomas distinguished himself at the hearings overall by claiming ludicrous blanks in his experience or recollections of it—this was known as the "stealth strategy"—and refusing to comment on what he considered private (Melone et al. 1992). Inconsistency in character meant ruin and madness in the *Times*. This was no doubt a discursive practice picked up from the quasi-judicial dramaturgy surrounding such public hearings.

But do any of us know ourselves sufficiently well to be able to find out whether the self we presume must be in there is consistent or not? At the end of the debate and after the vote, the *Times* did report some thoughtful musing on whether any nominee could stand up to such scrutiny of character, though the presumed ground for skepticism was much more probably the existence of original sin than the nonexistence of the continuous self (Carrithers et al. 1985; Elster 1986).

How one constructs a narrative in the present about the past was also bound to be an analytically interesting issue: the terms and assumptions of the present are not exactly identical to those of the past, and those who judge competing accounts in the present are, or ought to be, in a quandary. Do they assess the seriousness of the situation according to the standards and circumstances of the past—and if so, whose? Or do they assess past events, recounted in a narrative of the present, according to standards and circumstances that obtain at the moment—and if so, whose? Is there a way of narrating the past in its own terms? Or does any account of the past, given in the present, read the present into the past by definition? This problem is obviously a general one in cultural politics, as so many group identities are constructed by individuals as individual identities from narratives of past victimization or domination. Indeed, this makes problematic the whole convenient framework that attempts to distinguish the present from the past. Perhaps the different presents in which we all live, and from which presumed points we look back on the past, are themselves a constructed residue of those pasts, and nothing more (see p. 3).

This raises the possibility that people of the supposed present and people of the presumed past are necessarily different, and living in different worlds. Interestingly, the women's eyes/men's eyes issue also arose and further complicated the situation. Perhaps the committee was simply in no position to judge Hill's narrative, because they could not or would not understand it. Perhaps the Senate itself, which was 98 percent male, would be in a similar position when the nomination came to the floor for a vote. Senator Joseph Biden, the committee chair, attempted to find a men's analogy for Hill's recounted experience of harassment by shifting to what seemed in his immediate context to be a safe transposition of gendered relations: "I wonder how many men there are, if in fact they were approached by a man on the job who was . . . , [who] had a different sexual preference than they do, I wonder how ready they would be to go open and say, 'By the way, my boss, that fellow up there, approached me'" (NYT, 14 October 1991). The presumption that vulnerability for heterosexual men comes, not from heterosexual women, but from homosexual men, is an interesting and revealing commentary on the dynamics of heterosexuality and its construction against a homosexual other (Connell 1993a).

Third, I hypothesize that symbols and simulacra will become analytically relevant (Baudrillard 1988). Hill and Thomas were said by the *Times* to have become symbolic: of the new feminist politics; of abused black women; of brave and lonely private individuals who confront the horrors of partisan mudslinging; of the advancement of black people into the highest offices of the land; of highly paid black professionals who adopt the conservative values of the white elite; of careerism in party politics and negative campaigning. Indeed, as I suggest below, their entrance into the world of the political symbolism could hardly have been naïve or accidental.

As the hearings progressed, Hill and Thomas became inscriptions of these ideas, and thus living symbols: Hill was thirteenth in an Oklahoma farm family and introduced numerous relations to the committee, testifying in simple, uncolorful terms; Thomas was the man of dignity, pushed beyond endurance, forced to speak out and earnestly preferring "the assassin's bullet" to his ordeal. In a sense they were copies without originals, or simulacra, as they had no models of themselves previously in those roles to copy; nor were they copying in exact terms anyone else, real or fictional, who had been in some similar situation. They became characters in a spontaneously generated theatrical and televisual event, as it was obvious that they had an audience to play to; and to play to an audience they needed and used a vocabulary of signs and signals surrounding themselves and emerging from themselves in multiple ways. They were neither wholly scripted nor completely unstudied; they improvised and were never short of advice (on which point the *Times* was, as ever, newsily thorough) (NYT, 15 October 1991). When Hill and Thomas became public, politicized figures their personae necessarily changed, and their own comments reveal that they knew this to be the case. In a sense they became different people.

Findings

The major finding of my research was not hypothesized in advance but was in fact a complete surprise, as is often the way in science. Against expectation, I discovered that interpretative methodology was self-consciously and sophisticatedly employed by participants in the *Times* narrative; that it was perceived as essential to participant strategies; and that the winning strategy—Thomas's—was successful, so it seems to me, because it multiplied narratives, different narratives about Hill.

This conclusion is, of course, speculative and in no way derived from such data as interviews and questionnaires directed at the senators who voted. The strengths and weaknesses of those methods are too well known to rehearse here. My point is that any such conclusions about human behavior are speculations constructed by researchers using interpretative methods, and that my conclusions are not necessarily worse for having interpreted the material in the *Times* rather than having interpreted material in surveys. What makes such speculations more or less useful has to do with the purpose of the research and the effect on the intended audience. Presumptions that researchers have an authoritative interpretation of their own questionnaires, which are themselves taken to be an accurate representation of some logical or causal sequence antecedent to human behavior, are almost self-deconstructing.

My reading of the Hill-Thomas hearings is that Thomas and his supporters (some of whom were women) employed inconsistent and contradic-

tory narratives about Hill as a present personality, whereas Hill and her supporters had but one narrative about Thomas, and that was set in the past.
Moreover, Hill had but one narrative about herself, which she and her supporters were unable to defend successfully against counterattack. Thomas
had a nonnarrative about himself and was allowed, to a surprising extent, to
get away with it. He lashed out in the present at Hill and was not pushed on
his own past to the same degree, virtually all of it having become blandly
private. Hill, by contrast, pushed what was conventionally defined as private
behavior (and worse, private behavior relating to herself) into the public
realm and was sternly policed for doing so. The discursive power of the traditional public man/private woman frame was readily apparent. One of the
advantages of this commonplace frame is that it figures in innumerable easily recognized and readily communicated narratives that are almost a short-
hand, and are in that way prime examples of the power of symbolic representation in politics.

I am not claiming that participants in the *Times* narrative (and I emphasize that other sources would provide overlapping and corroborative
accounts) employed interpretative methodologies as methodologies, as such
methodologies are employed here. Rather, I am saying that participants hit
upon political strategies that were self-consciously interpretative. This is in
a sense an instance of mudslinging or negative campaigning, which is nothing new in practice or theory. But some of the participants in the *Times* narrative—the Thomas group—were unusually good at it.

Of course, we cannot know exactly why the Senate votes fell as they
did; indeed, I doubt that we can know with certainty why anyone does anything. We can merely produce more or less plausible accounts, and the criteria for plausibility will be lodged with one's readers. My conclusion that a
strategy of narrative multiplication was crucial in producing an outcome—
the Senate vote to confirm Thomas's nomination—is itself a speculation, as
intentional explanations always are, even when given by the agent in question. But I think it highly plausible, and rather more persuasive than commonplace accounts based on various interests ascribed to individuals, which
they are presumed to be pursuing. Such interests as there are, are also necessarily contextualized as narratives by those who hold and pursue them.
But not all narratives have to arise out of, or match up with, any pregiven or
contemporaneously developed interests. Good stories can grab you.

Narrative

By the time Hill and Thomas reached the committee room, media exposure,
as recounted in the *Times,* had effectively set the stage: the hearings would
be a courtroom drama and a TV sitcom, two genres to which the presumed

mass audience could respond. Committee hearings are at most only quasi-judicial and lack a presiding judge; effectively, all participants are partisan and can behave in a relatively informal manner. Jokes, anecdotes, and coziness abounded, as did flat contradiction, mixtures of counterclaim and question, and a general sense of improvisation in the absence of clear rules and precedents. It could have been scripted, it was taped and transcripted, and it will doubtless be dramatically reconstructed on television and in the movies. Yet, the dignity of the chambers, the sense of high office and responsibility, and the general dramaturgy of a trial, albeit by ordeal, made the televised venue a courtroom in which spectators could play at being jurors, evaluating evidence and judging credibility. There are certainly numerous models for the genre on U.S. network TV (Grant 1992).

The disjunction between what the judicial frame requires and the quasi-judicial frame permitted provides a striking theater of contrasts, incongruities, and tensions founded in uncertainty about "what ever would happen next." Hence, audience concern, as portrayed in the *Times,* was not wholly bound up with an unknown conclusion, but was also focused second-by-second on what genre would be invoked, and what narratives and symbols employed, by those speaking. The continuing ambiguity over what exactly were the rules of decorum gave the event an unusual edginess.

Narrative strategies played to two genres—courtroom drama and TV sitcom—creating flashback tales and novelistic characterizations. Actual trials, courtroom drama, and TV sitcoms are no great distance from each other, anyway. Each borrows elements from the other, and there is a circle of referential narrative out of which individuals, whatever their roles—jurors, actors, spectators—come to the interpretative understandings that they do, and the discursive strategies that they employ. It is no wonder that Hill-Thomas became one of those collective moments of historic voyeurism when the electronic screen links the activities and narratives of the nation, and of course the *Times* portrayed it in those terms while it was happening (Luke 1989).

Thomas and his supporters on the committee and elsewhere hit back at Hill to save his nomination. They did this by multiplying their portrayals of her character in order to impugn her credibility, that is, "someone like that could not have been telling the truth." From that sort of comment it was supposed to follow that Thomas was never guilty of sexual harassment and gross hypocrisy, and that therefore he was qualified to be associate justice of the Supreme Court. Thoughtful writers in the legal and jurisprudential community had already written, and still maintain, that he was distinctly unqualified for such a professional elevation and that his judicial record and legal abilities were never properly scrutinized (Dworkin 1991).

In person and by affidavit, Thomas and his supporters portrayed Hill as a hardheaded, determinedly rational careerist who could never have been so

innocently vulnerable a victim of sexual harassment. They also suggested
that she was the victim of erotomania, a syndrome of obsessive and inexplicable sexual attraction undeterred by rebuff. She was also given to fantasies and zombielike behavior, even schizophrenia, according to some testimony and comment in the *Times*. She was said to have stolen fictions from
popular books like *The Exorcist* (a self-referential inversion of their own
methodology) and to have pilfered facts from obscure legal cases. When she
passed a polygraph test, this was interpreted as further proof that her "flat-
out perjury" was so comprehensive that she believed the lies herself.
According to the Thomas camp, she was vindictive and attention seeking,
not the reserved, religious, and deeply private person she claimed to be.
Moreover, her use of consultants and media advisers was described as slick
and calculating, and her motivation for coming forward could only have
been political, according to her political detractors. She was said to be the
tool of special-interest groups with narrow agendas, stopping at nothing in
order to achieve some minority political goal. She was even portrayed as a
Joker, the character in the Batman film, garishly made up but grotesquely
deformed, grinning insanely at destructive pranks and glorying in the agony
of victims (NYT, 14–15 October 1991).

No one could have been all those things at once, and indeed, no one
added them up in order to evaluate their credibility, consistency, and plausibility. Piecemeal denial played into the strategy; as Hill said, every fifteen
minutes there was a new theory. One of the crucial elements in her defeat
was her surprise at this, and another was the failure of her supporters on the
committee to put Thomas through anything similar. After the Senate voted
fifty-two to forty-eight to confirm Thomas, the Democrats were derided in
the press as political wimps and closet chauvinists for failing to round on
Thomas with defamatory characterizations. As Machiavelli (1970, 278)
noted in his *Discourses,* the scrupulous fall victim to the wicked.

Had the Hill camp seen the narrative assault for what it was, they could
have identified it before the battle was lost. That would at least have given
them a choice concerning their scruples and tactics. Possibly they should not
have behaved differently, but possibly exposure of the tactics of the opposition would have vitiated some of its strength. As it was, Thomas successfully claimed that he was the victim of what can only be described as "reputation rape." This has the disturbing implication that he successfully played
the "Tootsie card": men are better at being women than women are, as the
movie vehicle for Dustin Hoffman seemed to imply. Indeed, the asymmetry
in valuation between narratives about men and those about women is a
major point of reference in my study here. Even man-as-victim and man-as-
woman can be positively "spun" to an audience, whereas positive narratives
about women are few by comparison, and negative ones extremely easy to

construct from the many stereotypes and clichés available in popular culture.

Thinking speculatively about the future, I would suggest that the prolif-
eration of modern media coverage makes it likely that narrative multiplication will become increasingly common, and that its use will be essentially
negative. Hillary Clinton is an obvious candidate. Against background
assumptions that probity is consistency, and that any and all allegations go
on the record and accumulate, the dominant strategy will become the multiple smear. Her changing hairstyles provided a useful symbolization of just
this process. As with individuals in the Hill-Thomas tale, so too with groups,
where individuals self-identify and encourage others to do so. Some years
ago Croatians were said to be winning the video war in the Yugoslav struggles; indeed, one graduate applicant to my department enclosed a tape—of
amateur, local TV, and CNN footage shot in Croatia—with his application to
study. World events and strategies of televisual representation do not always
remain out there.

Power

Fictions are what authors tell us; truths are fictions we tell ourselves repeat-
edly; they are truthful because they work—one way or another. Thomas
won, so I speculate, by invoking multiple truths that took hold precisely
because they were such good fictions. Not all propaganda succeeds; but if
you are on the receiving end, you need a strategy.

The Hill team would have done well to read *Advise and Consent* (Drury
1959), the political novel in which scandalous allegations of communism
and homosexuality emerge in and around fictional confirmation hearings in
the U.S. Senate, and then to develop a strategy that responded creatively to
the undoubted power of the smear. This is narrative power, and there were
plenty of ways to attack Thomas without stooping to quite the same level of
bizarrerie. The Thomas supporters offered plenty of hostages to fortune. He
was said to have been a devotee of pornographic films while at Yale, and his
character witnesses pursued an interesting line: they argued that Hill was not
generally credible because she had professional and sexual ambitions that
were just as basely meretricious as—their own! The Thomas camp churned
out narratives from the docudrama, the TV soap, and the miniseries; the Hill
team stuck repetitiously to integrity, understatement, and good taste. Even
that was undermined by snide references from the Thomas camp to certain
well-exposed failings among Hill's supporters—Senator Ted Kennedy and
the "bridge up in Massachusetts" was the most telling instance (NYT, 15
October 1991).

The Hill team followed academic values, the values of scholarly distance and unemotional veracity. But this presentation did not play in Peoria, where most senatorial minds are and must be, owing to the various publics that they feel they have to satisfy. If democracy is founded on mass representation and close communication between representatives and electorates, then there can be no great distance between the allusions, tropes, and narratives of politicians on the one hand and voters on the other. Indeed, there is every reason for the discourse and lifeworlds of the two to draw closer together, otherwise they would not understand one another. Some of the ordinary, working-class interviewees of the *Times* were women who thought that Hill should have dealt with whatever problem there was herself, just as they had or would, or so they said. Doubtless this made sense—within their own frame, of course—to the middle-class males on the committee (NYT, 15 October 1991).

Had Hill been more forthcoming in her self-characterizations, she could possibly have tipped the scales. Narrative models for the strong but vulnerable, ambitious but principled, feminine yet successful woman are thin on the ground. If there were more feminist novelists, and much more feminist life, Hill would have had a better chance, as she could have appealed to powerful narratives to support her credibility. The same is true for the Afro-American identity, hence the popularity of the novel *Roots* (Haley 1976), which provides a positive narrative about slavery and a picture of life before victimization. Indeed, it provides a cultural history for the previously historyless. There might also be ways through representation of politicizing the largely unspoken class divide in U.S. politics, other than the commonplace and divisive (but all-prevailing) narratives of individual success through competition (which do not deal at all well with losers).

Conclusion

Popular culture, from which such narratives derive, is not uniform; nor does it guarantee that subjects within it live in anything like the same world. What we can do in political theory is to confront what popular culture, despite its partial consistencies, has constructed as normal, as positive, and as other, and follow the logic of the dramaturgies that are characteristically employed. What happens when we do this depends on who we are and what we want to do. This "we" is too often merely presumed in political theory; contextual location and dialogical intent, by contrast, are strategies available to theorists that respect individuals and open possibilities. Theorizations that explicitly (or more usually implicitly) prioritize presumed identities—for example, black over poor over Muslim over woman over lesbian over mother over disabled (or whatever!)—are necessarily complicit with some interests rather than others. There is no escaping complicity, but it ought to be carefully examined and justified, and the consequences (for whom?) made visible.

Political theory does not have to be the politics of fighting back; but it is no bad thing to be ready to fight back. Presumedly meaningful differences and politicized hierarchies of power and esteem are well established in society. The zones of exclusion and negative evaluation are already in place, and it is difficult, as noted above, to find ways that individual and collective reevaluations can succeed against the stereotypes and clichés. Political theory that is complicit with these stereotypes and out of dialog with those who are marginalized and excluded seems highly suspect to me. The interpretative strategies I have adopted seem well adapted to making these things visible, and dialog actually possible.

It does not follow that every self- or group evaluation that runs against stereotype is by definition good or tolerable within such democratic arrangements as can be found. But such justifications as there are for the exclusions and evaluations that are taught and rewarded in society should not be based on the narratives of the natural, the inevitable, the universal, and the good that feminists and others have been so laboriously deconstructing. The strategic advantages that are gained through complicity with these constructions (e.g., in linking feminism to an essentialist view of woman, or gay men's politics to an essentialist view of homosexual) all buy into visibility at the price of conservatism concerning the very factors that created the problems (Vance 1992; Evans 1993). Moreover, the interrelationships, indeed codefinitions, of supposedly basic categories—gender, class, race/ethnicity, and so forth—need to be followed through the complex dialogs and symbolic performances of constructed political events, such as the *Times* version of the Hill-Thomas hearings of 1991. That way we can understand how politics is done, and how to do it better.

In undertaking this exercise I argued that class, race/ethnicity, religion, language use, and other cultural phenomena are interdefined with the characteristics of sex and sexuality. Though the characteristics of sex and sexuality are almost always framed with essentializing and naturalizing narratives, my reading of the literature, discussed in Chapter 1 (see pp. 15–16, 22–24), is that analytically there are advantages to treating them all as linguistic constructions that are mapped, in various ways, onto bodies and ascribed to identities. I take this view because sex and sexuality are not only alterable through medical technology and choice, but also because they are not really stable categories of biology or identity in the first place, precisely because the finer points of meaning, which arise as these terms are used, are crucially important politically and highly variable with context. What becomes visible and obvious through using a category like *woman* or *black/Afro-American/Afro-Caribbean* merely masks a variety of further assumptions in subtexts. Naturalizing and essentializing discourses are thus further attempts to keep these subtexts invisible, and they do this by functioning as symbolic markers for convenient assumptions and silences. This is precisely why the political and theoretical battles over the implications of *Ain't I a Woman* and *Am I that Name?* (hooks 1982; Riley 1988) have been so important. Rather than conceptualizing "woman" or "masculinity," for example, as a kind of personalized yet common essence that manifests itself somewhat differently among individuals in society, I am arguing that the disadvantages inherent in excessive abstraction (e.g., the individual as universal subject; see pp. 28–32, 35–36) are best addressed not by reinscribing the barriers of essentializing or naturalizing discourse (strategically in practice or theoretically in ideas), but by dismantling them. They should be dismantled because they overspecify similarity and institutionalize difference. Similarity and difference are themselves too variable—with individual choice, cultural heritage, life-cycle variation, and innumerable other considerations—to be disciplined by such crude terms. It is up to people to discover commonalities that they find relevant to the politics they want to do, whereas it is not for some individuals to determine in advance what meanings others are allowed to create, particularly by telling them who and what they are and are not. It is through such linguistic moves that some attempt to arrogate power to themselves and deny it permanently to others.

Much the same is true of the narratives within popular culture, as these are ways of representing people (generally by way of characters and stereotypes) that distribute power in hierarchies. This is because they are regularly invoked by actors in politics, among which I include the press. On the one hand, this is the language of democracy, because it is literally demotic, but on the other hand, it is a repository of power relations, particularly ones that, for example, privilege men and disadvantage women. Popular culture is a mélange of genres that influences politics, because politics in a democratic society is characteristically constructed through these images and stories, which have to be familiar. Yet this area has not been much considered in political theory until recently, despite the fact that political theory is itself an attempted intervention into politics—at a certain level, and in a certain way. These interventions might be more successful if they were constructed in a practical conjunction with demotic language, and if politics itself were characterized more persuasively as a demotic project. Theorists might thereby be in a better position to influence their own popularizations, and thus be more effective in what they are trying to do.

My investigation of the Hill-Thomas hearings as an episode in gender politics is not a study of a woman on the political stage, as I have argued all along that gender is not a synonym for women, though what she did, and what happened to her, could well be an alternative and persuasive reading. Rather, my account was intended to be a case-study interpretation of how

sex and sexuality become power relations in society. To do this, I characterized Thomas and Hill as actors (in both the political and the thespian senses) because they appealed to the images and allusions they felt their audience would understand. Their language and self-presentation (as represented
through the medium of the *Times*) revealed the variety and complexity
inherent in the way that commonplace categories of sex, sexuality, and
race/ethnicity were deployed by the (apparent) principals, although the
Times inscribed its own Manichaean dualisms and character norms of consistency. However, the *Times* also demonstrated the democratic character of
the event by recording citizens' interpretations of it. Though these articles
were themselves an event, the paper frames itself as a mirror, and I have subverted this by alluding to what everyone knows, namely that the *Times* is
widely read on Capitol Hill. Thus, my study broadens the notion of an event
in politics to fit a politics of interpretation that is democratic by definition.

The way that class occurs as a theme in citizens' comments, but not in
the self-representations of the actors, illustrates the extent to which commonplace characterizations (lawyer, professional) mask other issues that citizens are themselves perfectly capable of teasing out. Conversely, the success of the Thomas camp in playing on commonplace stereotypes (to Hill's
disadvantage) illustrates both the ease with which a range of silences and
subtexts (otherwise known as smears and innuendo) can be deployed, and
the massive difficulty any effective deconstruction must face.

What struck me as new in the Hill-Thomas episode in terms of gender
(ways that sex and sexuality become power relations in society) was how
private man was put on stage. Thomas's attempts to keep the substance of
the allegations about his predatory heterosexuality out of bounds did not
succeed, and part of the intense public fascination with the whole episode
might be put down to the novelty involved—the "Long Dong Silver" inter-
change comes particularly to mind. The supposed division between the public and the political, on the one hand, and the private and the personal, on the
other, could not be sustained, and it will be even more difficult to maintain—for those who want to—in the future. Putting private woman on the
public stage was very effective in getting private man up there, too, and the
resulting negative scrutiny of dominant masculinity is now on the record. Of
course, there are different ways of interpreting the record, but the feminist
and gender-critical readings have arguably gained in visibility and plausibility (see pp. 110–113).

How power accumulates around heterosexual men—in a manner that is
indifferent (at least sometimes) to race/ethnicity, religion, and other categories—was dramatically illustrated in Hill's confrontation with an all-male
committee and an overwhelmingly male Senate. The political effects of
making that apparatus of masculine power highly visible were immediate,
and are now available for reinscription in the political record. While it is

depressing that gender politics was played out in such a dirty way, the fact that it was played at all in gender terms (the use of sex and sexuality to victimize and abuse in practice and through representation) is perhaps heartening. What the episode did not reveal in any detail is how dominant masculinity rests on categorial exclusions and disciplinary practices that affect men as well, and interlock with class oppression. Although these considerations did surface in the *Times,* the chances that they will creep off the page and into popular politics seem slight. For that to happen, a new and different cast of characters would have to come forward, and a politics of interpretation would need to (de)construct it.

In my concluding chapter, I review the relationship between the explicatory techniques employed in this book and the interpretative politics of gender that emerges.

Conclusion

I have, in this book, undoubtedly promised more than I have delivered. My defense for this is that no one could deliver on all the promises, once and for all, and that no work of theory delivers anything in other than theoretical terms, anyway. But there is value in raising questions in order to disturb the generally smooth surface of academic theorizing, and in particular to challenge some of the unquestioned assumptions about the genre and narrative strategies typically employed to get these ideas across. Pursued to an illogical extension, this kind of deconstructive activity shatters such few communicative possibilities as there may be even at the best of times, but I hope that I have not trespassed on anyone's sanity to quite that extent.

In writing this book, I have used techniques of textual and narrative analysis within a mild form of postmodernism. However, as there are no grand confrontations with modernity, the Enlightenment, postmodernity, or hyperreality in my text, it is very likely that this postmodernism merely represents a way of handling language that some readers—the hermeneutically inclined—will find commonplace. That is perfectly fine with me. My ambitions lie in looking carefully at language: not taking tropes unconsciously, noticing how metaphor is used to create meaning, and confronting the writer-audience nexus (Shapiro 1985–1986; Ball 1995).

The incorporation of a gendered perspective on men into political theory is the particular project of this work. But this is a complex matter. On the one hand, a gendered perspective on men, and on their masculinity as dominant and pervasive, has been generated by feminists within feminist theory. I argue that it is time for mainstream/malestream theory to take this whole perspective much more seriously, and not to leave it somewhere on the margins intellectually and professionally. On the other hand, a gendered perspective on men, as generated within the sociology of masculinities, and rather more historically and discursively within men's studies, tends to make men and their masculinities more varied in terms of domination and subordination within the male group, as well as with respect to women. Rather than theorizing this as a collapse of feminist identity (defined against the monotonic, monolithic, and yet paradoxical degendered male as other), I have suggested that politically and theoretically there is considerable room for negotiating agendas and building alliances. Private man is a public matter, and the complexities of the issues are now coming out, as are new and complex political alignments.

Rather than set this up as men's politics/women's politics binary, I have chosen to broaden the concept of gender to cover the ways that sex and sexuality become power relations in society. To do that I have worked through a classic discussion of "the family" (in Chapter 2), the typical biographical characterization of "a life" (in Chapter 3), and an episode in the historical recovery of relationships that were variously familial, sexual, and friendly (in Chapter 4). It is an atypical though not unknown feminist strategy to foreground men in such discussions, and my overall aim was to make men even more problematic. Another important way of doing this is to draw attention to the silences of the texts of mainstream/malestream political theory, and to the feeble symbols that actually appear there, as I do in Chapter 1. Both traditional writing and conventional reading function to make debate seem unthinkable or unnecessary concerning how power is distributed in society through the complexities of gender, and I have attempted to subvert this.

The historical material through which my explorations of this web of gendered power relations has proceeded may seem somewhat remote (like Marx and Engels) or arbitrary (like Hill and Thomas) to many readers. My defense is that theory needs illustrative material and conceptual practices against which to work. Moreover, I did not think that my discussions would make much sense unless I disarranged the presumptions from which theory is usually written, and so I attempted to expose the way that theory relies on biography, and then criticized the ways that biographies are usually constructed. In addition I have challenged the conceptualization of my explorations as "merely historical" by attempting to collapse the present into the past, in order to give my narrative the immediacy of nearby experience. Moving from the world of Marx and Engels to the Hill-Thomas hearings (as I do in Chapter 5) is thus not so much a shift to the present as a shift from the enduring greats of political theory to the evanescent icons of the "mediacracy." Their story may or may not attain much currency over the years, but as further evidence for the complex character of gender politics, it is nearly ideal.

Discursively, I adopted varied and contrasting trajectories: in Chapter 1 I confronted the abstractions of political philosophy and sociology in order to do political theory; in Chapter 2 I worked from a classic text back to the author; in Chapter 3 I moved from a life of the author back to famous texts; in Chapter 4 I connected biographers to narratives; and in Chapter 5 I linked narratives in popular culture to democratic politics through the media. This schematic summary is intended to demonstrate that authorial strategy, very little considered in the literature on political theory (never mind within it), is alive and well and on the agenda.

Thus, I have argued that many boundaries that are apparently firm, particularly the ones that give a familiar structure to life, are really movable metaphors that generate realms of power. And I have added that the pretense that these boundaries are immovable is itself a source of further power. These conceptions are not new (Shapiro 1986; Butler 1990), but I have tried to push their use in new directions. Rather than direct them outward beyond the margins of conventional sexualities, I have directed them inward toward heterosexual masculinities and the family. Rather than see them as methodological tropes reflecting a (supposedly) postmodern world, I have turned them backward toward the conceptual worlds of theory and contextually related worlds of biography that had previously seemed over and agreed. Moreover, I have asked the reader of the classics of political theory to attend to the textual flickering of the universal subject between masculine and degendered personae, and the noticing and silencing entailed in the symbolic deployment of fatherhood in classic works. As I deploy a concept of the lifeworld, applicable to theorist, commentator, biographer, and subject alike, the family is not merely a site where sexuality and domesticity mingle, but also a site where the class struggle is confronted by the middle and working classes, where friendships are made and tested within gender boundaries, and where the extended family, even if not often present, can wield a powerful influence. I see no reason why an impoverished account of the lifeworld should be visited on theoretical and biographical subjects (such as Marx and Engels) in the rarefied world of political theory, whether it is textually conducted through abstraction and illustration, or through contextualization and explication. In practice, of course, the lifeworld is constructed on the spot, and I have looked at one account—the *Times* on Hill and Thomas—and speculated on how this was done in a political context saturated with popular culture, rather than theoretical abstractions.

I hope that I have convinced those who do not normally attend conferences and workshops (which political theorists consider a normal activity) that political theory as a genre is itself an interesting way to raise practical problems in conceptual terms. Of course, it may be that what I am doing will not be readily recognized as political theory, though personally I think that I have made innumerable concessions to the genre. I hope that there is just enough left of it to get my point across, and that political theory as an activity will be the better for relaxing its form and broadening its content. There might even be some real politics in it, as in these matters the microlevel of power relations is not to be despised or overlooked, though it is certainly not the only level on which to struggle. I have argued that there are commonalities of the lifeworld shared by theorists, classic authors, and political actors, and that men and masculinity/ies are so normal and so obvious there that we do not even see them most of them time, at least not in a broadly analytical and politically critical sense. I hope that there are ways in which political theory, suitably reinterpreted as a complex narrative construction, can contribute to the subversion of the oppressions that men create through their power over women, and their use of gender in society.

References

Abramson, Jill et al. 1992. New Voice. *Wall Street Journal,* 20 March.

Alexander, Jeffrey C. 1987. The Centrality of the Classics. In *Social Theory Today,* edited by Anthony Giddens and Jonathan Turner. Cambridge: Polity Press.

Anderson, Benedict R. 1991. *Imagined Communities: Reflections on the Origin and Spread of Nationalism.* London: Verso.

Arblaster, Anthony. 1984. *The Rise and Decline of Western Liberalism.* Oxford: Blackwell.

Bacchi, Carole L. 1991. *Same Difference: Feminism and Sexual Difference.* Sydney: Allen & Unwin.

Ball, Terence. 1995. *Reappraising Political Theory.* Oxford: Oxford University Press.

———, ed. 1987. *Idioms of Inquiry.* Albany: State of New York University Press.

Barrett, Michèle. 1983. Marxist Feminism and the Work of Karl Marx. In *Marx: 100 Years On,* edited by B. Matthews. London: Lawrence & Wishart.

———. 1985. Introduction to *The Origin of the Family, Private Property and the State,* by Friedrich Engels. Harmondsworth: Penguin.

———. 1992. Words and Things: Materialism and Method in Contemporary Feminist Analysis. In *Destabilizing Theory,* edited by Michèle Barrett and Anne Phillips. Cambridge: Polity Press.

Barrett, Michèle, and Anne Phillips, eds. 1992. *Destabilizing Theory.* Cambridge: Polity Press.

Baudrillard, Jean. 1988. *Selected Writings.* Edited by Mark Poster. Cambridge: Polity Press.

Benhabib, Seyla, and Drucilla Cornell, eds. 1987. *Feminism as Critique: Essays on the Politics of Gender in Late-Capitalist Societies.* Cambridge: Polity Press.

Berlin, Isaiah. 1978. *Karl Marx: His Life and Environment,* 4th ed. Oxford: Oxford University Press.

Bleicher, Josef. 1980. *Contemporary Hermeneutics.* London: Routledge.

———. 1981. *The Hermeneutic Imagination.* London: Routledge.

Blumenberg, Werner. 1972. *Karl Marx: An Illustrated Biography.* Translated by Douglas Scott. London: New Left Books.

Bly, Robert. 1990. *Iron John: A Book about Men.* Reading, Mass.: Addison-Wesley.

Bock, Gisela, and Susan James. 1992. *Beyond Equality and Difference: Citizenship, Feminist Politics and Female Subjectivity.* London: Routledge.

Borges, Jorge Luis. 1987. Pierre Menard, Author of the Quixote. In *Labyrinths.* Harmondsworth: Penguin.

Bottomley, Gill, Marie de Lepervanche, and Jeannie Martin. 1991. *Intersexions.* Sydney: Allen & Unwin.

Boyne, Roy, and Ali Rattansi. 1990. *Postmodernism and Society.* Basingstoke: Macmillan Education.

Braidotti, Rosie. 1987. Envy: Or with Your Brains and My Looks. In *Men in Feminism,* edited by Alice Jardine and Paul Smith. New York: Methuen.

Brittan, Arthur. 1989. *Masculinity and Power.* Oxford: Blackwell.

Brod, Harry, ed. 1987. *The Making of Masculinities: The New Men's Studies.* Boston: Allen & Unwin.

Brod, Harry, and Michael Kaufmann. 1994. *Theorizing Masculinities.* Newbury Park, Calif.: Sage.

Brown, Wendy. 1987. Where is the Sex in Political Theory? *Women and Politics* 6:3–23.

———. 1988. *Manhood and Politics: A Feminist Reading in Political Theory.* Totowa, N.J.: Rowan & Littlefield.

Burke, Peter, ed. 1991. *New Perspectives on Historical Writing.* Cambridge: Polity Press.

Butler, Judith. 1987. Variations on Sex and Gender: Beauvoir, Wittig and Foucault. In *Feminism as Critique,* edited by Seyla Benhabib and Drucilla Cornell. Cambridge: Polity Press.

———. 1990. *Gender Trouble: Feminism and the Subversion of Identity.* London: Routledge.

———. 1993. *Bodies that Matter: On the Discursive Limits of "Sex."* London: Routledge.

Callinicos, Alex. 1987. *Making History.* Cambridge: Polity Press.

Carrigan, Tim, Bob Connell, and John Lee. 1985. Toward a New Sociology of Masculinity. *Theory and Society* 14:551–604.

Carrithers, Michael et al. 1985. *The Category of the Person: Anthropology, Philosophy, History.* Cambridge: Cambridge University Press.

Carver, Terrell. 1983. *Marx and Engels: The Intellectual Relationship.* Brighton: Harvester Press and Bloomington: Indiana University Press.

———. 1989. *Friedrich Engels: His Life and Thought.* London: Macmillan and New York: St. Martin's Press.

———. 1992. Marx, Engels and European Democracy: 1848/1989. *Political Theory Newsletter* (Canberra) 4:130–137.

Cockburn, Cynthia. 1983. *Brothers: Male Dominance and Technological Change.* London: Pluto Press.

———. 1988. Masculinity, the Left and Feminism. In *Male Order: Unwrapping Masculinity,* edited by Rowena Chapman and Jonathan Rutherford. London: Lawrence & Wishart.

———. 1991. *In the Way of Women: Men's Resistance to Sex Equality in Organizations.* Basingstoke: Macmillan.

Connell, R. W. 1987. *Gender and Power: Society, the Person and Sexual Politics.* Cambridge: Polity Press.

———. 1990. The State, Gender, and Sexual Politics. *Theory and Society* 19:507–544.

———. 1993a. A Bastard of a Life: Homosexual Desire and Practice among Men in Working-class Milieux. *Australia and New Zealand Journal of Sociology* 29:112–135.

———. 1993b. The Big Picture: Masculinities in Recent World History. *Theory and Society* 22:597–623.

Connell, R. W., and G.W. Dowsett, eds. 1993. *Rethinking Sex: Social Theory and Sexuality Research.* Philadelphia, Penn.: Temple University Press.

Coole, Diana H. 1993. *Women in Political Theory: From Ancient Misogyny to Contemporary Feminism,* 2d ed. Boulder: Lynne Rienner and Brighton: Harvester/Wheatsheaf.

―――. 1994. Whither Feminisms? *Political Studies* 42:128–134.

Crowley, Helen, and Susan Himmelweit. 1992. *Knowing Women: Feminism and Knowledge.* Cambridge: Polity Press in association with the Open University.

Dallmayr, Fred. 1987. Political Inquiry: Beyond Empiricism and Hermeneutics. In *Idioms of Inquiry,* edited by Terence Ball. Albany: State of New York University Press.

Delmar, Rosalind. 1977. Looking Again at Engels's "Origins of the Family, Private Property and the State" In *The Rights and Wrongs of Women,* edited by Juliet Mitchell and Ann Oakley. Harmondsworth: Penguin Books.

Dietz, Mary. 1992. Context Is All: Feminism and Theories of Citizenship. In *Dimensions of Radical Democracy,* edited by Chantal Mouffe. London: Verso.

di Stefano, Christine. 1991. *Configurations of Masculinity: A Feminist Perspective on Modern Political Theory.* Ithaca, N.Y.: Cornell University Press.

Drury, Allen. 1959. *Advise and Consent.* Garden City, N.Y.: Doubleday.

Dunn, John, ed. 1992. *Democracy: The Unfinished Journey, 508 B.C. to A.D. 1993.* Cambridge: Cambridge University Press.

Dworkin, Ronald. 1991. Justice for Clarence Thomas. *New York Review of Books* 38 (7 November).

Elshtain, Jean Bethke. 1981. *Public Man, Private Woman: Women in Social and Political Thought.* Oxford: Martin Robertson.

―――. 1986. *Meditations in Modern Political Thought: Masculine/Feminine Themes from Luther to Arendt.* New York: Praeger.

―――. 1987. *Women and War.* New York: Basic Books.

Elster, Jon. 1986. *The Multiple Self.* Cambridge: Cambridge University Press.

Engels, Frederick. 1980. *The Origin of the Family, Private Property and the State.* In *Selected Works in One Volume,* by Karl Marx and Frederick Engels. London: Lawrence & Wishart and Moscow: Progress Publishers.

Enloe, Cynthia. 1990. *Bananas, Beaches and Bases: Making Feminist Sense of International Politics.* Berkeley: University of California Press.

Evans, David T. 1993. *Sexual Citizenship: The Material Construction of Sexualities.* London: Routledge.

Evans, Judith. 1986. *Feminism and Political Theory.* London: Sage.

Family Correspondence [of Marx daughers]. 1984. Translated by Faith Evans. Harmondsworth: Penguin.

Ferguson, Kathy E. 1984. *The Feminist Case Against Bureaucracy.* Philadelphia, Penn.: Temple University Press.

―――. 1991. Interpretation and Genealogy in Feminism. *Signs* 16:322–339.

―――. 1993. *The Man Question: Visions of Subjectivity in Feminist Theory.* Berkeley: University of California Press.

Filene, Peter. 1987. The Secrets of Men's History. In *The Making of Masculinities,* edited by Harry Brod. Boston: Allen & Unwin.

Foucault, Michel. 1984–1988. *History of Sexuality.* 3 vols. Translated by R. Hurley. Harmondsworth: Penguin.

Gatens, Moira. 1991. *Feminism and Philosophy.* Cambridge: Polity Press.

―――. 1992. Power, Bodies and Difference. In *Destabilizing Theory,* edited by Michèle Barrett and Anne Phillips. Cambridge: Polity Press.

Gemkow, Heinrich et al. 1972. *Friedrich Engels: A Biography.* Dresden: Verlag Zeit im Bild.

Gibbons, Michael T. 1987. Interpretation, Genealogy and Human Agency. In *Idioms of Inquiry,* edited by Terence Ball. Albany: State of New York University Press.

Giddens, Anthony. 1979. *Central Problems in Social Theory: Structure and Contradiction in Social Analysis.* London: Macmillan.

———. 1982. *Profiles and Critiques in Social Theory.* London: Macmillan.

———. 1987. *Social Theory Today.* Cambridge: Polity Press.

Grant, Judith. 1989. Gender as a Category in Feminist Theory. Paper presented to the Western Political Science Association, Salt Lake City, Utah, 30 March–1 April.

———. 1992. Prime Time Crime: Television Portrayals of Law Enforcement. *Journal of American Culture* 1992:57–68.

———. 1993. *Fundamental Feminism.* New York and London: Routledge.

Grimshaw, Jean. 1986. *Feminist Philosophers: Women's Perspectives on Philosophical Traditions.* Brighton: Wheatsheaf Books.

Haley, Alex. 1976. *Roots.* Garden City, N.Y.: Doubleday.

Haraway, Donna. 1991. *Simians, Cyborgs, and Women: The Reinvention of Nature.* London: Free Association Books.

Harding, Sandra. 1992. The Instability of the Analytical Categories of Feminist Theory. In *Knowing Women,* edited by Helen Crowley and Susan Himmelweit. Cambridge: Polity Press in association with the Open University.

Hartsock, Nancy. 1983. *Money, Sex and Power: Toward a Feminist Historical Materialism.* New York: Longman.

Hearn, Jeff. 1987. *The Gender of Oppression: Men, Masculinity and the Critique of Marxism.* Brighton: Wheatsheaf Books.

———. 1992. *Men in the Public Eye: The Construction and Deconstruction of Public Men and Public Patriarchies.* London: Routledge.

Hearn, Jeff, and David Collinson. 1994. Unities and Differences between Men and between Masculinities. In *Theorizing Masculinities,* edited by Harry Brod and Michael Kaufmann. Newbury Park, Calif.: Sage.

Hearn, Jeff, and David Morgan, eds. 1990. *Men, Masculinities and Social Theory.* London: Unwin Hyman.

Henderson, W. O. 1976. *The Life of Friedrich Engels.* 2 vols. London: Frank Cass.

Hobbes, Thomas. 1991. *Leviathan,* edited by Richard Tuck. Cambridge: Cambridge University Press.

hooks, bell. 1982. *Ain't I a Woman: Black Women and Feminism.* London: Pluto Press.

Jonásdottír, Anna. 1991. *Love Power and Political Interests.* Örebro: University of Örebro; also published as *Why Women Are Oppressed.* Philadelphia, Penn.: Temple University Press, 1994.

Jones, Kathleen B. 1990. Citizenship in a Woman-Friendly Polity. *Signs* 15:781–812.

———. 1993. *Compassionate Authority.* New York: Routledge.

Kapp, Yvonne. 1972–1976. *Eleanor Marx.* 2 vols. London: Lawrence & Wishart.

Kennedy, Ellen, and Susan Mendus. 1987. *Women in Western Political Philosophy.* Brighton: Wheatsheaf Books.

Kimmel, Michael S. 1987. The Contemporary Crisis of "Masculinity" in Historical Perspective. In *The Making of Masculinities,* edited by Harry Brod. Boston: Allen & Unwin.

Krader, Lawrence. 1972. Introduction to *The Ethnological Notebooks of Karl Marx: Studies of Morgan, Phear, Maine, Lubbock.* Assen: Van Gorcum and New York: Humanities Press.

Lavoie, Don. 1990. *Economics and Hermeneutics.* London: Routledge.

Leacocke, Eleanor Burke. 1981. Introduction to *The Origin of the Family, Private Property and the State,* by Frederick Engels. London: Lawrence & Wishart.
Lloyd, Genevieve. 1984. *The Man of Reason: "Male" and "Female" in Western Philosophy.* London: Methuen.
Locke, John. 1988. *Two Treatises of Government.* Edited by Peter Laslett. Cambridge: Cambridge University Press.
Luke, Timothy W. 1989. *Screens of Power.* Urbana and Chicago: University of Illinois Press.
Machiavelli, Niccolò. 1970. *The Discourses.* Edited by Bernard Crick. Harmondsworth: Penguin.
MacKinnon, Catharine. 1987. *Feminism Unmodified: Discourses on Life and Law.* Cambridge, Mass.: Harvard University Press.
McLellan, David. 1973. *Karl Marx: His Life and Thought.* London: Macmillan.
———. 1990. The Pursuit of Contradiction. *The Times Higher Education Supplement,* 23 February 1990.
Mann, Thomas. 1988. *The Magic Mountain.* Harmondsworth: Penguin.
Marcus, Steven. 1974. *Engels, Manchester and the Working Class.* New York: Random House.
Martin, Jeannie. 1991. Multiculturalism and Feminism. In *Intersexions,* edited by Gill Bottomley, Marie de Lepervanche, and Jeannie Martin. Sydney: Allen & Unwin.
Marx, Karl. 1986. *Capital.* Vol. 1. Translated by Ben Fowkes. Harmondsworth: Penguin and London: New Left Review.
Marx, Karl, and Friedrich Engels. 1956–1968. *Werke.* Berlin: Dietz Verlag.
———. 1970. *The German Ideology: Part One,* edited by C. J. Arthur. London: Lawrence & Wishart.
———. 1976–. *Collected Works.* (series incomplete). London: Lawrence & Wishart.
———. 1980. *Selected Works in One Volume.* London: Lawrence & Wishart and Moscow: Progress Publishers.
Melone, Albert et al. 1992. Too Little Advice: Senatorial Responsibility and Confirmation Politics. *Judicature* 75:187–192.
Mendus, Susan. 1992. Losing the Faith: Feminism and Democracy. In *Democracy,* edited by Joahn Dunn. Cambridge: Cambridge University Press.
Mill, John Stuart. 1989. *On Liberty.* Edited by Stefan Collini. Cambridge: Cambridge University Press.
Modleski, Tania. 1991. *Feminism without Women: Culture and Criticism in a Post-feminist Age.* New York: Routledge.
Morgan, David H.J. 1981. Men, Masculinity, and the Process of Sociological Enquiry. In *Doing Feminist Research,* edited by H. Roberts. London: Routledge & Kegan Paul.
———. 1992. *Discovering Men: Sociology and Masculinities.* London: Routledge.
Morrison, Toni, ed. 1992. *Race-ing Justice, En-gendering Power: Essays on Anita Hill, Clarence Thomas, and the Construction of Social Reality.* New York: Pantheon.
Mouffe, Chantal, ed. 1992. *Dimensions of Radical Democracy: Pluralism, Citizenship, Community.* London: Verso.
Murphy, John W. 1989. *Postmodern Social Analysis and Criticism.* New York: Greenwood.
Nicholson, Linda J., ed. 1990. *Feminism/Postmodernism.* London: Routledge.
Nye, Andrea. 1989. *Feminist Theory and the Philosophies of Men.* New York: Routledge.

Okin, Susan Moller. 1979. *Women in Social and Political Thought.* Princeton, N.J.: Princeton University Press.

Pateman, Carole. 1988. *The Sexual Contract.* Cambridge: Polity Press.

Pateman, Carole, and Teresa Brennan. 1979. Mere Auxiliaries to the Commonwealth. *Political Studies* 27:183–200.

Pateman, Carole, and Elizabeth Gross. 1986. *Feminist Challenges: Social and Political Theory.* London: Allen & Unwin.

Pateman, Carole, and Nancy Hirschmann. 1992. Political Obligation, Freedom and Feminism." *American Political Science Review* 86:179–188.

Petersen, V. Spike, ed. 1992. *Gendered States: Feminist (Re)Visions of International Relations Theory.* Boulder: Lynne Rienner.

Petersen, V. Spike, and Ann Sisson Runyan, eds. 1993. *Global Gender Issues.* Boulder: Westview.

Pettman, Jan. 1991. Racism, Sexism and Sociology. In *Intersexions,* edited by Gill Bottomley, Marie de Lepervanche, and Jeannie Martin. Sydney: Allen & Unwin.

Phelan, Shane. 1989. *Identity Politics: Lesbian Feminism and the Limits of Community.* Philadelphia, Penn.: Temple University Press.

Phillips, Anne. 1991. *Engendering Democracy.* Cambridge: Polity Press.

———. 1992a. Universal Pretensions in Political Thought. In *Destabilizing Theory,* edited by Michèle Barrett and Anne Phillips. Cambridge: Polity Press.

———. 1992b. Must Feminists Give Up on Liberal Democracy? *Political Studies,* special issue on "Prospects for Democracy." 40:68–82.

Pimlott, Ben. 1991. Winston—Messiah in the Nick of Time. *The Guardian,* 4 April.

Pringle, Rosemary. 1993. Absolute Sex? Unpacking the Sexuality/Gender Relationship. In *Rethinking Sex,* edited by R. W. Connell and G. W. Dowsett. Philadelphia, Penn.: Temple University Press.

Pringle, Rosemary, and Sophie Watson. 1992. "Women's Interests" and the Post-Structuralist State. In *Destabilizing Theory,* edited by Michèle Barrett and Anne Phillips. Cambridge: Polity Press.

Raddatz, Fritz J. 1978. *Karl Marx.* Translated by Richard Barry. London: Weidenfeld & Nicolson.

Riley, Denise. 1988. *"Am I that Name?" Feminism and the Category of "Women" in History.* London: Macmillan.

Ryan, Michael. 1988. Postmodern Politics. *Theory, Culture and Society* 5:559–576.

Said, Edward W. 1985. Opponents, Audiences, Constituencies and Community. In *Postmodern Culture,* edited by Hal Foster. London: Pluto Press.

Sayers, Janet, Mary Evans, and Nanneke Redclift, eds. 1987. *Engels Revisited: New Feminist Essays.* London and New York: Tavistock Publications.

Scheppele, Kim Lane. 1989. Foreword: Telling Stories. *Michigan Law Review* 87:2073–2098.

Scott, Joan. 1991. Women's History. In *New Perspectives on Historical Writing,* edited by Peter Burke. Cambridge: Polity Press.

Seery, John. 1990. *Political Returns: Irony in Politics and Theory from Plato to the Anti-Nuclear Movement.* Boulder: Westview.

Segal, Lynne. 1990. *Slow Motion: Changing Masculinities, Changing Men.* London: Virago.

Seidler, Victor J. 1991a. *Recreating Sexual Politics.* London: Routledge.

———, ed. 1991b. *The Achilles Heel Reader.* London: Routledge.

Shanks, Michael, and Christopher Tilley. 1987. *Social Theory and Archaeology.* Cambridge: Polity Press.

Shapiro, Michael J. 1985–1986. Metaphor in the Philosophy of the Social Sciences. *Culture and Critique* 2:191–214.

———. 1986. *The Politics of Representation.* Madison: University of Wisconsin Press.

Singer, Peter. 1980. *Marx.* Oxford: Oxford University Press.

Skinner, Quentin. 1988. A Reply to my Critics. In *Meaning and Context,* by James Tully. Cambridge: Polity Press.

Spender, Dale. 1982. *Women of Ideas and What Men Have Done to Them: From Aphra Benn to Adrienne Rich.* London: Routledge & Kegan Paul.

Squires, Judith. 1993. Reviews of *Dimensions of Radical Democracy,* edited by Chantal Mouffe and *Engendering Democracy,* by Anne Phillips. *Feminist Review* 44:120–123.

———. 1994. Private Lives, Secluded Places: Privacy as Political Possibility. *Environment and Planning D: Society and Space* 12:387–401.

Stevens, Jacqueline. 1993. Leviticus in America: The Politics of Sex Crimes. *Journal of Political Philosophy* 1:105–136.

Stiehm, Judith. 1983. *Women and Men's Wars.* Oxford: Pergamon Press.

———. 1984. The Man Question. In *Women's Views of the Political World of Men,* edited by Judith Stiehm. Dobbs Ferry, N.Y.: Transnational Publishers.

Tickner, J. Ann. 1992. *Gender in International Relations: Feminist Perspectives on Achieving Global Security.* New York: Columbia University Press.

Tully, James. 1988. *Meaning and Context: Quentin Skinner and His Critics.* Cambridge: Polity Press.

Vance, C. S. 1992. Social Construction Theory: Problems in the History of Sexuality. In *Knowing Women,* edited by Helen Crowley and Susan Himmelweit. Cambridge: Polity Press in association with the Open University.

Vogel, Lise. 1983. *Marxism and the Oppression of Women: Toward a Unitary Theory.* New Brunswick, N.J.: Rutgers University Press.

Walby, Sylvia. 1990. *Theorizing Patriarchy.* Oxford: Blackwell.

———. 1992. Post-Post-Modernism? Theorizing Social Complexity. In *Destabilizing Theory,* edited by Michèle Barrett and Anne Phillips. Cambridge: Polity Press.

Weeks, Jeffrey. 1985. *Sexuality and Its Discontents: Meaning, Myths and Modern Sexualities.* London: Routledge & Kegan Paul.

West, David. 1989. *Authenticity and Empowerment: A Theory of Liberation.* Brighton: Harvester/Wheatsheaf.

White, Hayden. 1987. *The Content of the Form: Narrative Discourse and Historical Representation.* Baltimore, Md.: Johns Hopkins University Press.

Wittig, Monique. 1992. *The Straight Mind and Other Essays.* Hempstead: Harvester/Wheatsheaf.

Wolff, Robert Paul. 1978. There's Nobody Here but Us Persons. In *Women and Philosophy: Toward a Theory of Liberation,* edited by Carol C. Gould and Marx W. Wartofsky. New York: Putnam's.

Young, Iris Marion. 1990. *Justice and the Politics of Difference.* Princeton, N.J.: Princeton University Press.

Zerilli, Linda M. G. 1994. *Signifying Woman: Culture and Chaos in Rousseau, Burke, and Mill.* Ithaca, N.Y.: Cornell University Press.

Index

About the Book

This wide-ranging collection of essays undermines two commonly held pre-conceptions: that "gender" means "women," and that feminist politics are of no concern to men.

Women's studies, feminist theory, and gender studies tend to present boundaries that inhibit communication: insiders speak to each other, and outsiders find it easy not to listen. Carver cuts across these traditional boundaries in his conceptualization of theoretical problems and political issues. He considers "malestream" theory and theorists, for example, from the perspective of a well-established feminist critique.

Linking political theory to the intellectual biographies that inevitably accompany it, Carver explores how exactly "the personal is political." He also examines the complex intertwining of gender with class and "race"/ethnicity and theorizes gender in relation to sex and sexuality. His book reveals familiar texts and authors in a new light, demonstrating the power and scope of the gendered perspective in political theory.

Terrell Carver is professor of political theory at the University of Bristol (England). His many publications include *Marx and Engels: The Intellectual Relationship; Friedrich Engels: His Life and Thought; Karl Marx: Later Political Writings;* and "Engels's Feminism" (in *History of Political Thought*).